P9-CND-716

More Man
than
You'll Ever Be

JOSEPH P. GOODWIN

More Man ☙ than You'll Ever Be

GAY FOLKLORE

AND ACCULTURATION

IN MIDDLE AMERICA

Indiana University Press

BLOOMINGTON & INDIANAPOLIS

© 1989 by Joseph P. Goodwin
All rights reserved

*No part of this book may be reproduced or utilized in any form or by
any means, electronic or mechanical, including photocopying and
recording, or by any information storage and retrieval system, without
permission in writing from the publisher. The Association of American
University Presses' Resolution on Permissions constitutes the only
exception to this prohibition.*

Manufactured in the United States of America

Library of Congress Cataloging-in-Publication Data

Goodwin, Joseph P.
    More man than you'll ever be : gay folklore and
acculturation in middle America / Joseph P. Goodwin.
    p. cm.
    Bibliography: p.
    Includes index.
    ISBN 0-253-33893-X. ISBN 0-253-20497-6 (pbk.)
    1. Gay men—United States—Social conditions. 2. Gay men—
United States—Folklore. 3. Gay men—United States—Social life and
customs. I. Title.
HQ76.2.U5G66 1989
306.7'662'0973—dc19   88-45461
                                                        CIP

1 2 3 4 5 93 92 91 90 89

Dedicated with love to my mother,
Mary B. Goodwin,
and to the memory of my father,
William P. Goodwin

CONTENTS

Acknowledgments

I have always been a bit put off by the pro forma lists of meaningless names in the acknowledgments included in books. Now that I find myself finishing this manuscript, I realize that the people and their names in such lists are anything but meaningless.

The original version of this study was my doctoral dissertation at Indiana University. My research committee—Mary Ellen Brown, John Wm. Johnson, James H. Justus, and Sandra K. Dolby-Stahl—through their comments and suggestions were most helpful in the completion of that version. Mary Ellen, as my director, helped me shape the manuscript into a well-organized work; her close reading and criticisms of content and style were invaluable. Susan Matusak and Jo Basey, who at that time worked at what was then the Alfred C. Kinsey Institute for Sex Research, were of great help in finding many of the resources I used.

The men I interviewed for this study were extremely open with me; they gave thoughtful and thought-provoking answers to my questions, and they continue to express an interest in my research. Without their contributions the examples cited would have been much less interesting.

Phillip M. Hoskins and Michael Jonson have been gracious hosts whenever I have needed a chance to get away from home. They are experts in the care and feeding of former Bloomingtonians.

Inta and Bruce Carpenter remain very special to me, as does Joseph P. Burford.

Gary Barker created the art for the cover, and David Abernathy took the photograph. I appreciate their help and friendship.

To those who have read and commented on this manuscript, especially Camilla A. Collins, Rayna Green, Sue Kiefer Hammersmith, Venetia Newall, and Polly Stewart, I am grateful.

Finally, I owe more than thanks to my family, especially my mother, Mary, for the moral, emotional, psychological, and financial support and the love they have given me.

Introduction

As I walked into the bar in New Orleans that fall evening in 1975, I felt as though my knees were going to give way before my stomach did. I was jittery with anticipation, curiosity, and fear. Once inside, my impressions were mixed: the bar appeared to be much like other bars I had been in, yet I felt awkward, unsure of myself, even out of place. There were no women present; the room was quite dark; the men seemed acutely aware of their surroundings and of each person who entered the bar. Only much later did I realize that the gay bar reflected a culture different from the one in which I was accustomed to operating and that this culture had its own language, traditions, and behavior codes that one needed to know in order to function comfortably and effectively within it. Thus it was no wonder that I was disoriented.

As I began to observe patterns of communication among gay people, I started wondering if there were a body of gay folklore, and if so, what it included and what purposes it served. After extensive involvement with the gay subculture in several cities, my thoughts suddenly began to gel. I realized that many, if not most, of the interactions that I had observed or in which I had participated were solidly based in traditions that are ubiquitous within the gay world. Moreover, it became apparent to me that this large segment of our society has been virtually (virtuously?) ignored by folklorists.[1]

This neglect is no longer justifiable. As we have continued to expand our concept of folklore, its functions, its methods, and its very nature, we have also realized that folklore is found among all groups and all social classes, within every culture and subculture. Homosexual people, according to most estimates, make up approximately ten percent of the population.[2] Although the gay subculture by no means includes all homosexual men and women,[3] it does embrace a large number of them. For this reason, gay folklore has become a significant aspect of urban folklore, and as such, deserves our attention.

In studying this material, I have chosen to use the word *gay* instead of *homosexual*. There are a number of justifications for this usage. First of all, *homosexual* is a relatively new word. It is made up of Greek *homo,* meaning "same" (not Latin *homo,* "man"), and Latin *sexus,* "sex," and was coined in the late nineteenth century and introduced into English by Havelock Ellis in 1897.[4] *Gay,* on the other hand, although its etymology is obscure, has a much longer history and is probably related to "the Provençal word 'gai' [which] was used in the thirteenth and fourteenth centuries . . . for an openly homosexual person."[5]

Moreover, *homosexual* is primarily a clinical term used to describe people who are physically attracted to members of their own sex; it is an "other" identification. Occasional homosexual acts may be performed by heterosexual people. *Gay*, however, is a self-identification, used consciously by those homosexual people who are accepting of their sexual orientation, but it extends beyond the mere sexual aspects of life.[6] Given these facts, and since this study is written from an insider's point of view, I believe that it is appropriate to use the terms *gay* and *homosexual* in the way that they are used by most gay people.

Numerous other words have been used to refer to gays, including *invert, sodomite, pederast, Uranian, queer, faggot, fairy, pansy, fruit,* and *queen.* These terms will appear in the following pages only in quotations or in references to the words and their usage. They vary in offensiveness, but even though words like *queer* and *faggot* are generally considered highly pejorative, they are sometimes used by members of the gay subculture as expressions of intimacy, inverting and altering the straight culture's connotations of them.[7] Grace Sims Holt describes a similar use of *nigger* among blacks.[8] As she explains,

In taking The Man's strongest weapon and using it to your advantage, you have denuded him of verbal power, and by implication freed yourself from the psychological bondage that "hate" labels impose. Freedom from the psychological bondage forces a change in power relations which pressures a drive from self-determination and status. Liberation begins with language.[9]

The gay subculture is made up of those homosexual people who have identified themselves as gay, who consider their orientation to be an important (but not totally defining) aspect of their lives, and who frequently interact with other gays *as* gays. The group I am classifying as the gay subculture is made up of those people included in Kenneth Plummer's fourth level of homosexuality, "homosexuality as a way of life." (Plummer's first level is "casual," with sexual relations being insignificant to the participants; the "personalized level" involves the homosexual person who does not associate with the subculture; and on an "institutional level" homosexuality serves as an outlet for persons temporarily cut off from heterosexual opportunities, people like prisoners, for example.)[10]

A subculture is generally a social phenomenon, an associational network. Usually a subculture will develop an argot, a private method of communicating, even when among outsiders; use of the argot also serves as a means of mutual identification and helps to foster subcultural cohesion. Although competent use of the language is not required for membership in the subculture, an understanding of it is almost inevitable, since constant exposure guarantees an acquisition—conscious or not—of the argot's meaning.

The subculture may also generate its own businesses that are supported by group members—such as the numerous gay establishments serving the gay community. In turn, the subculture may come to rely upon some of its own businesses for support. Gay bars, for example, serve as gathering places for the gay community. Subcultures would exist, however, even without the presence of such organizations, because they arise out of social forces that are independent of all institutions. Cultural pressures from the mainstream—reprobation, stigmatization, and rejection—result in alienation and isolation. Persons experiencing these feelings and who have identified themselves as different, deviating from the norm, seek out others of their own kind. As the subculture begins to coalesce, its members develop their own sense of values. These standards often will run contrary to those of the main society; frequently they are inversions or distortions of the larger culture's norms.[11] Finally, each member of the subculture is an individual and may hold values more in line with the mainstream, more radical than those of the subculture, or anywhere on a continuum in between.

Much has been written on homosexuality during the last twenty-five years or so, but the cultural studies have concentrated on large cities, especially New York and San Francisco, where there are long-established gay communities, businesses, and organizations. More recently major gay communities have emerged in such cities as Chicago, Dallas, Houston, and Atlanta.

In the cities one can choose from many political, activist, and social groups in which to participate. There he or she can find friends, role models, teachers, and support. In the smaller towns, however, one's options are much more limited. In one small midwestern city, for example, gay men and lesbians have three organizations that they can join: a university group (not an appealing choice for older men and women or for those not affiliated with the university), a religious group that is quite small and very "cliquish," and a professional group, which requires that its members be college graduates or own businesses. These groups combined serve fewer than one hundred people in a town that statistics tell us should have more than ten thousand lesbians and gay men. Thus it is very difficult for someone just "coming out" to find his or her niche.

In the smaller cities and towns, the opportunities for gay living remain for the most part covert. The bars and other gay spaces are easy to find—in fact, rather widely known even outside the gay community—yet they are essentially esoteric spaces outside of which one's homosexuality is seldom if ever revealed. Political issues are largely ignored; it is still dangerous to speak out. In most such towns, the only activities related to homosexuality that most gay men and lesbians are involved in are social or sexual. Stonewall is not widely known; Harvey Milk and Dan White, if people have heard of them at all, are unremembered. Even the tragedy of AIDS has yet to really hit home in middle America.

The majority of American gay men live in this sort of social climate. The "culture" of New York and San Francisco does not play a major conscious part in the lives of gay men in much of the country. To overemphasize coastal gay culture would skew any study of gay life, and yet that is what has been done. Because of the previous research on these parts of the country, much of the material in this study may seem dated. I can only say that it was current when I collected it, primarily in 1981 and 1982.

Some major topics may seem to be missing, especially sexual lore. A subculture that is based to a great degree on the sexual identity of its members will of course have generated an extensive body of sexual folklore. I may be faulted for not including that material in this study, but I have two reasons for omitting it. First, I tried to keep a narrow focus and chose a limited range of material for consideration. Second, I consider sexual traditions to be primarily a part of sexual enculturation, which is a process separate from acculturation to the subculture. One need not be sexually enculturated to function competently in the gay community.

Because of its covert nature, the gay community lacks the formal institutions that usually assist in enculturation. The family, churches, schools, and social organizations all take part in teaching people how to operate in the straight culture. The media also function in heterosexual enculturation: there are innumerable "teenagers in heat" movies, other love stories on film and television, and "mainstream" romance novels. Only recently, however, have gay topics been dealt with, and not always sensitively. Lesbianism has been almost completely ignored, and it will continue to be neglected until we understand that women are just as relevant to the world as men are. The media have far, far to go.

Without comparable sources of instruction and support, gay people must rely primarily upon each other to learn how to function effectively within the gay world. Much of this information is passed on in the form of folklore. Acculturation, however, is an extremely complex process, and folklore is only one of the mechanisms involved; no doubt anthropologists and sociologists could specify numerous other factors that play a part in attaining cultural competence.

Drawing from four major types of gay folklore—verbal and nonverbal communication, humor, drag (female impersonation), and personal experience narratives—I seek to show how such traditions serve the gay subculture as means of communication and identification, as an aid to subcultural cohesion, and as ways of coping with conflict both within the subculture and between the gay community and the straight world.

The relationships among communication, identification, cohesion, and conflict are complex. Identification can take place only after some communication, yet in a stigmatized subculture communication is inhibited until tentative identification of other members takes place. Similarly, cohesion is built upon a sense of commonality and belonging, thus following (when it occurs) from communication and identification. Cohesion results in a support system for coping with conflicts between the subculture and the majority culture. At the same time conflict reinforces cohesion, causing people to unite when facing a common foe. Conflict can also occur within the subculture when members perceive themselves to be substantially different from each other.

One such source of conflict within the community is drag. Many activists feel that drag is politically incorrect since it reinforces stereotypes and since it can be interpreted as chauvinistic. Others feel that drag is passé. But if one examines such gay men's travel guides as the annual *Bob Damron's Address Book* and the advertisements in the many gay community papers and magazines around the country, one can clearly see that drag shows are still very common and popular. And since drag *is* so closely associated with stereotypes and is so visible, and since it is a unique sort of behavioral genre, I think it is important that it be included in this study.

The unexplored richness of the folklore of the gay subculture cannot be denied; nor should it be overlooked any longer. The gay community is an important urban phenomenon, and, as such, its traditions must be included in folklorists' considerations of the vastness of folk culture.

More Man
than
You'll Ever Be

❦ 1

Coming to Terms

ESTABLISHING A PERSPECTIVE

PARTICIPATION IN THE GAY subculture is essentially a leisure-time activity.[1] There are exceptions, of course, particularly in larger cities where gay people may work in gay businesses, eat in gay restaurants, shop in gay stores, attend gay parties and churches, and live in gay neighborhoods. For the most part, however, gay people tend to divide their time between the gay subculture and the larger, more visible straight culture.

This division of time, of work and leisure, is made necessary by the straight culture's inability to cope with people different from "the norm," in short those people who are often viewed by the majority as deviant. Meredith R. Ponte has suggested that "'deviance' is but an extension of 'normalcy.'"[2] Most people, however, do not see deviance as normal; in fact the word *deviance* carries strong negative connotations, although its denotative meaning is primarily concerned with difference rather than with value judgment. Because we generally equate "different" with "bad," we tend to view those who are not like us as inferior, evil, or perhaps perverted. As John Boswell has succinctly pointed out, "Majorities . . . create minorities, in one very real sense, by deciding to categorize them."[3] He also shows that, in terms of homosexuality at least, such has not always been the case. The classical Greeks and Romans did not make distinctions between heterosexuality and homosexuality, because neither condition seemed more natural nor more remarkable to them than did the other.[4]

Members of the white male culture, however, seem to have a need to create oppositions. They perceive things in polarities, and indeed many items, concepts, and actions fit such a pattern. We are comfortable with this sort of balance: it fills a need for a sense of completion or resolution; it allows us to view life in terms that parallel "good" and "evil." Thus the notions of masculine men and feminine women require the development of the opposing concepts of effeminate men and masculine women. (As Vito Russo states, "The idea that there was such a thing as a real man made the creation of the sissy inevitable."[5])

This tendency to see oppositions is one motivation behind the creation of stereotypes. Logically we must ask why we would create such categories, since they often represent types of behavior considered wrong by many people. The perceived impropriety of effeminate men and masculine women is necessary to justify and underscore the "rightness" of feminine women and masculine men. If there is no formulated concept of "wrong," the concept of "right" is weakened considerably. And, as Ruth Benedict has said, "Modern man, differentiating into Chosen People and dangerous aliens, . . . has the justification of a vast historical continuity behind his attitude."[6]

Creation, then, of these stereotypes gives the majority a convenient way of categorizing—regardless of accuracy—homosexual men and women. Since the straight culture generally considers homosexual people to be wrong at best, homosexuality has been stigmatized. In fact, any person whose same-sex orientation is discovered risks being subjected to all of the stigma imposed by the larger society in concentrated form, because he or she must serve as a scapegoat for many more people whose homosexuality remains hidden. Even those gay people who are not publicly recognized as such, however, suffer from both the stigmatization and the fear of discovery. This shared fear serves as a bond among gay people.[7] It is a common link within the gay subculture, and in fact is probably the forge in which the chain of bondage and brotherhood was made.

Being forced to form a secret system for interacting and for meeting people similar to themselves meant that gays also had to develop a private means of communication,[8] which in turn fostered a heightened sense of community. Rejected by the larger culture, gay people turned to their subculture, which—especially through its folklore—could serve as a source of strength and as a way of developing a surrogate system of social support.

The gay subculture is marginal to the larger straight culture, although most gay people function within both. Feeling segregated because of rejection and stigmatization by straights, gays have in effect intensified their isolation by choosing to associate primarily with other gay people, an act resulting in self-segregation. Therefore one must assume that gay people, a stigmatized, dynamic, yet basically invisible group, have created a set of shared traditions. In spite of these facts, folklorists have until recently failed to acknowledge the existence of this group, with its rich esoteric traditions and about which an easily accessible exoteric folklore has developed.

As William M. Hoffman points out, the gay subculture has been a historical reality for centuries; it is not simply the remnant of a political movement of the 1960s.[9] Boswell has shown that gay subcultures have existed for at least two thousand years, with varying degrees of visibility. Beginning in the fourteenth century the subculture in Europe, faced with increasing hostility, went "underground," not to become really visible again until recent years.[10]

In the United States the gay liberation movement grew out of the subculture early in the twentieth century and was composed of very small groups primarily in New York and in California. Although these organizations did not accomplish a great deal themselves, they were the basis underlying the later movement. The 1950s and 1960s saw an expansion of these groups, and in 1969 gay liberation was born. When police raided the Stonewall Inn in Greenwich Village in June 1969, investigating alleged illegal liquor sales, a handful of gays fought back. The Stonewall Riot continued for three nights and is now commemorated nationally every summer.[11]

Stonewall was not the only force behind the new struggle. Edmund White suggests that increasing urbanization and the decreasing economic necessity of families assisted in the development of both gay and women's liberation.[12] The counterculture of the 1960s also played a role in gay liberation, as did the civil rights movement. Gays adopted and adapted many of the tactics used by these groups.[13]

The liberation movement has made the gay subculture more visible and thus more accessible. As a result, much has been written about homosexuality during the last two decades. Little of this research, however, has focused on the important role folklore plays as those gay men who join the subculture pass through a series of identifiable stages. The process is, for the most part, linear, although in some instances the sequence is altered. People being acculturated always have the option of ending their subcultural involvement, a termination that can occur at any point. In addition, considering the complexity of acculturation, it is impossible to state that any given person has been fully acculturated. After the initial period of exposure and learning, the process may slow down a great deal, but it never ceases altogether unless the person experiencing it curtails his membership in the community.

There are five major steps a man faces in gay acculturation: (1) he identifies himself as gay; (2) he decides to associate with other gay people ("the gay community," "the gay subculture"—his concept of who these people are may not yet be well thought out); (3) he associates with the subculture for the first time; (4) he begins to learn the information necessary for efficient functioning within the subculture; and (5) through the competence he has gained at the previous stage, he begins to serve as a model or teacher for others entering the subculture.

Although sexual activity may occur at any point during acculturation, it is not per se a part of the process, nor is it required in order for one to become acculturated. Similarly, within the straight culture, sexual acts are not generally learned as one is enculturated. Homosexual activity, therefore, should probably be considered within a framework of sexual enculturation rather than subcultural acculturation. (Sexual enculturation would include such stages as becoming sexually aware; learning techniques through reading, discussing with others, attending sex education classes, watching pornographic movies, and practicing; becoming adept; and teaching others.)

Self-identification, the first level of gay acculturation, is usually a realization that people reach by themselves, although on occasion someone may guide a person through this step. Identification and the first association with the subculture—the third stage—are both coming-out events, in which the gay man first reveals his homosexuality to himself, and then to other members of the gay community. Other instances of coming out, such as to one's family and friends, are essentially semiprivate acts and as such are only incidental to the acculturation process. Levels one and three are also related in another way. Many homosexual people may spend much of their time in the gay world without really being aware of their own sexual orientation. When these men do become aware of their homosexuality, they reach level one *after* level three.[14] If a person does not progress beyond the first level, he is more properly termed a homosexual man than a gay man.

The second and third stages may occur almost simultaneously, or they may be quite separated in time. Often a person undergoes a period of adjustment between deciding to investigate the subculture and getting up his courage to do so. The fourth stage, learning, begins at the moment level three has been achieved. At this point the newly emerged gay man begins to choose—consciously or unconsciously—whether to use the language, adopt the values, and carry on the traditions of the subculture. If a person becomes an active bearer of gay folklore,[15] then step five is inevitable. Even if he does not choose to be a model for men entering the subculture, his use of the material will be observed and taken in by others, an occurrence over which he has virtually no control. After all, much traditional learning is an osmotic process in that information is absorbed unconsciously rather than being formally studied. Only later does the person realize that he himself has knowledge that he previously witnessed others use.

As one passes through stages four and five, he learns many traditions, some of which fall into a number of recognized genres; other clearly folkloric material and behaviors, like drag and camp, do not. For example, humor pervades gay folklore; indeed humor even suffuses the argot. One result of this ubiquitous humor is that some material seems to fall completely outside generic categories.

Barre Toelken makes the point that

one of the key features of a folk group will always be the extent to which its own dynamics continue to inform and educate its members and stabilize the group. Because the members share so much information and attitude, folk groups are what Edward T. Hall would call *high context groups*: For them, meaning and action are more directly related to context than to simple denotations of words themselves.[16]

The gay subculture is one such high context group, and this tight relationship of meaning, action, context, and folklore also contributes to the problem of making generic distinctions.

With these points in mind, we can examine folklore as a multifaceted process that functions in many ways. Traditions help to hold the subculture together and in many cases express the gay community's differences from the straight culture, defining the in-group based on an understanding of its folklore and a sharing and acceptance of subcultural attitudes.

The important relationship for gays among meaning, action, and context makes it difficult to grasp the functions of gay folklore without considering in great detail the themes present in the material. Just as context and tradition are inseparable, function and meaning are tied to context. Indeed, for gay folklore—if not for all traditions—function is the result of theme plus context (both real and perceived). Each one depends upon, gives to, and takes from every other one.

For example, suppose some gay men at a party are telling jokes. One of them asks, "Do you know what the difference between a killer whale and a bull dyke is? About fifty pounds and a flannel shirt." Although this joke expresses conflict, in context it is serving primarily as entertainment, as well as partially defining the in-group by insulting a category of people who are from some points of view outsiders. Therefore the joke functions primarily as a cohesive mechanism. On the other hand, if it were told among men in a gay bar where a lot of women were present, this same joke could express resentment of the sexually integrated nature of the bar. Joking about the women, and by extension their presence, could help to relieve tension, thereby serving as a socially acceptable alternative to open hostility or even violence. In this instance the joke could function as a means of coping with conflict. Finally, if this joke were told to the women themselves, it would very likely trigger a great deal of anger, in which case the joke would be functioning to promote conflict. Thus, a change in context can result in a change in function even though the theme remains constant.

Perception further complicates the progression from performance to function (and then to action, which could range from another performance to distancing oneself from the situation to physical violence). The process can be outlined in this way: performer's intended theme and perceived context filtered through audience's perceived theme and perceived context results in function. Therefore, the actual function may be quite different from the intended function.

The role of perceived context in folklore analysis cannot be dismissed. In recent years folklorists have placed an increased emphasis upon the study of folklore within its proper cultural context, feeling that tradition cannot be fully understood without considering situational factors attendant upon it. As Dan Ben-Amos points out, "For the folkloric act to happen, two social conditions are necessary: both the performers and the audience have to be in the same situation and be part of the same reference group."[17] This point of view is fine, as far as it goes. Unfortunately it overlooks the possibility of the simultaneous existence of multiple perceptions of a single "folkloric act." This oversight is probably the result of our tendency to define contexts in terms of such observable phenomena as persons present, physical setting, time frame of the event, and performance style. One of the strongest forces affecting a folkloric act, however, is the performer's mind set, his or her definition of the situation. One's perception of what is taking place is a strong determinant in the choice of items for presentation, the way in which they are used, and the way that she or he interprets the performances of others.

Dell Hymes has stressed that ethnographies of communication must "keep the multiple hierarchy of relations among messages and contexts in view."[18] Other writers have underscored the fact that different people will perceive the same situation in various ways.[19] Kenneth Plummer gives the following example:

> The student, John, was a "homosexual" and was "known about" by one particular heterosexual friend, Bill. . . . He was walking down a corridor at his college with Bill, when he saw a young man walking by whom he "fancied." He swung his head around as the attractive stranger walked by, and he commented that he "fancied that." Bill . . . swung his head around but couldn't see anybody in the corridor.
> . . . Subsequently Bill realized that John was referring to the other man, and that there was no woman in the corridor. The same objective situation—three men in a corridor—thus took on quite different meanings according to the symbolic world of the actor.[20]

Erving Goffman, drawing upon the work of Gregory Bateson, has developed the concept of frame analysis as a means of dealing with this phenomenon. For example, he points out that "a 'couple' kissing can also be a 'man' greeting his 'wife' or 'John' being careful with 'Mary's' makeup."[21]

Thus we see that an understanding of the actor's definition of the situation is crucial to the interpretation of the folklore. Moreover, it is possible for one person to perceive a given situation in more than one way. As Alf H. Walle has shown, some people considered the diner in which Walle did his field work to be simultaneously an eatery, a social center, and a sexual marketplace.[22] Although some perceptions may be held on a more conscious level than others, they all affect the performer's use of folklore and they must all be considered in analyzing the material. By using such an approach we may find that a single joke may be functioning as entertainment, as a means of getting attention, as a way of impressing a waitress in order to ensure prompt service and special treatment, and as a prelude to a sexual proposition. In other words, context, perception, and function are interdependent and therefore inseparable.

With the existence of personal multiple definitions of a given situation, we are faced with the possibility of people with different perceptions of the context interacting with each other. For example, in a gay bar it is traditional to offer only one's first name in meeting another person. (This practice is at least partially the result of a fear of outside acquaintances finding out about one's homosexuality. Many people, however, do give their full names, perhaps as a means of defying the secrecy imposed upon them by the straight culture.) If one man, considering the situation to be a sexual marketplace, introduces himself by first name to someone who has defined the context for himself as being primarily social and who therefore responds with his full name, the results of the interaction may be interpreted by the first man as a sign of openness; as an indication that the other man is unfamiliar with gay behavior codes and may be new to the gay world; as a breach of bar etiquette; or even as a warning that the person to whom he is talking is one who—in revealing his name—is seeking more personal information than he has a right to know. On the other hand, the fact that the second man gave his full name may have no significance at all to the first. Before we can really understand the depth of this brief interaction, the messages conveyed and the messages received, we must ascertain the perceptions of the context held by the people involved. To say that they were two men meeting in a gay bar in Bloomington, Indiana, on a Wednesday evening in September 1981 is insufficient information for an accurate analysis to be made of the interaction.

Misinterpretation is not the only problem that may result from people interacting from different contextual perceptions. Sally Yerkovich states, "A misused conversational genre can embarrass where we intend to praise, can divide where we intend to unify, and can turn a social situation upside down."[23] Misuse can result from differing definitions of the situation as well as from ignorance. Worse than causing embarrassment, incongruent perceptions can create conflict. According to Toelken, writing about obscene folklore, some messages can be considered inappropriate when conveyed to the wrong audience.[24] Walle mentions that sometimes a pretended conflict occurs when someone aware of the intended message of a folklore performance refuses to acknowledge that message and chooses to interpret the information from a different situational point of view.[25]

Some people even take advantage of multiple perceptions, using them to manipulate behavior. According to Walle, some performers use humor to explore other people's openness to sexual liaisons without actually making propositions.[26] Plummer writes about gay men who put on a gay act that allows them to touch and flirt with other men in such a way that the audience interprets the behavior as mere play.[27]

This sort of manipulation also gives the actor an opportunity to transform the situation from one level to another. Yerkovich writes about the use of such phrases as "I'm not very good at telling jokes" to "change the situation from that of joke telling where the competent performance is expected to that of reporting a joke."[28] In the same way, as Walle's article on using jokes as sexual propositions illustrates, a joke can be used to shift the perceptions from situation to situation.[29] And since they are inextricably bound together, a change in situation will result in a change in function.

The two examples that follow will illustrate the relationships between function and multiple perceptions of the context.

In September 1981 I attended a party with a number of other graduate students in folklore. Shortly after arriving I began a conversation with one of the other men present. Upon learning that he was from a city known for its gay population and that he had worked in a job associated with gay men, I mentally drew upon familiar stereotypes and thought, "Hm, he might be gay." When he learned that I was doing research on gay folklore, he said I should go to his hometown to do field work. We then began talking about that city and a number of its gay bars.

Soon a joke-telling session began. There was a core group of about eight people present; others wandered in and out. My new acquaintance, Fred, asked if I knew what gay termites eat. When I said that I did not know, he responded, "Woodpeckers." Over a period of about two hours a wide variety of jokes were told, mainly dealing with sexual, ethnic, racial, and gay themes. Fred, a female member of the group, and I were the most active participants. In addition to the jokes, numerous double entendres were exchanged. Knowing the great value placed by gays upon verbal agility, I frequently looked over at Fred to check his reactions. I also noticed that he was often doing the same with me, especially whenever he used a double entendre containing what I took to be a gay reference. He would occasionally drop gay terms into the conversation, words like *dishing,* meaning "gossiping" or "insulting."

Later in the evening we were both standing against a counter. My hand was resting on the edge of the counter and he was leaning against it. One of the first rules a gay man learns is not to move away when touched by another man; the corollary to this rule is, when touched by a man, touch him back in response. (This rule is generally phrased, "Don't move, or move back.") This process is used to help determine whether the other man is gay. Fred did not move away after touching my hand; though I left my hand in position, I did not make the contact any more substantial.

The party lasted about five hours. During that period Fred and I frequently exchanged glances, jokes, and comments. I decided that he must be gay. I interpreted the things he said, his behavior, his responses to my comments, and numerous other bits of circumstantial information as being strong indicators of homosexuality. His familiarity with things gay was truly convincing.

Later, when I asked about his orientation, Fred said he was straight. How did I manage to make this mistake after such an extended period of interaction? Fred and I were operating with different definitions of the situation. I can easily identify five perceptions that I held: (1) a party; (2) strangers getting acquainted; (3) folklore graduate students discussing folklore research and other topics of mutual interest; (4) a joke-telling session; and (5) an exploration of Fred's sexual orientation. Fred, on the other hand, was probably defining the situations as being only the first four. Thus I was interpreting his communications from several points of view, one of which was invalid. In other words, I was inferring information that he had not implied. Whereas folklore was functioning for me as a way of breaking the ice, a means of showing my knowledge, an attention-getting mechanism, entertainment, and an aid to determining another person's sexual orientation, for Fred this last use, at least, was not a consideration.

The next example is based on the following series of joking questions, which I was asked in the spring of 1980. The questions were spread over several weeks, heightening their effect by causing them to seem unrelated. The teller presumably had at least two purposes in mind: to entertain me and others present, and to share some humor with me, knowing my love of jokes.

What's the difference between a nun and a woman taking a bath?
One has hope in her soul.

What's the difference between a pickpocket and a peeping Tom?
One of them snatches watches.

What's the difference between a women's track team and a group of clever pygmies?
One's a bunch of cunning runts.

Do you know what the difference between a blow job and lunch is?
Good. Let's go have lunch.

Taken as a single entity, these jokes can function in several ways simultaneously, assuming that the appropriate situational definitions are present. One of the most obvious functions is to entertain. By telling the jokes the narrator can evoke laughter from the person or group to which he has told it. Among the side-effects of this laughter are a feeling of importance and satisfaction on the part of the teller, who has succeeded in getting and holding the attention of an audience. The shared experience of hearing the jokes, understanding the homosexual implications of the fourth question (when told by one male to another), and laughing at the person who falls into the carefully laid trap all serve to enhance the sense of unity within the group. Thus the jokes increase the notion of in-group, fostering cohesion.

On a less blatant level, the jokes can function as a means of communication and identification, conveying—when considered within the social context and together with other jokes being told—that the teller might be gay. The listeners' responses, then, can provide a similar indication of their orientations. "Let's go!" or some such answer (given, of course, in a joking or semijoking manner) would suggest that the respondent may be gay and that the subject should be pursued further. On the other hand, if responses are limited to laughter and groans, which communicate little more than appreciation of the jokes, the teller has learned nothing of the listeners' sexual orientations.

The unanticipated change in form of the fourth question allows another possible use. The humor in the first three questions is linguistic, being based upon spoonerisms mentally supplied by the listener in the first and third and upon an understood transposition of words in the second. In the last question, however, there is a surprise change. The question is similar to a catch riddle, putting forth to the listener, who is caught off guard, an unexpected proposition. Even in a group situation, this final joke is usually directed toward a particular person. Although the proposition is rendered in a joking manner, it *can* be intended seriously, serving as a foundation upon which more suggestive remarks can be laid, further intensifying signals of the teller's sexual interest in the listener.

Given the multiplicity of coexistent perceptions affecting any event and the diverse levels of meaning that can be connected to these perceptions, it is clear that folklorists must broaden their perspectives in order to improve their analyses. Thus they must go beyond a stated interest in contexts to a recognition of multiple definitions of the situation and their impact upon the functions of folklore. To do so, folklorists must also be aware of denotative meanings so that they can understand the ambiguities and connotations that allow people to shift contexts easily and quickly. Only then can folklorists suggest the richness and complexity of the material they study.

ᗺ 2

It Takes One to Know One

COMMUNICATION AND IDENTIFICATION
IN THE GAY SUBCULTURE

WE ARE CONSTANTLY being bombarded by innumerable signals; we are, after all, sentient beings, and as such we receive messages in many ways. Not only do we interpret what we see and hear; odors, flavors, and physical sensations also have a bearing on our understanding of our environment and the information it contains. Virtually everything communicates. Confronted with so many messages, we filter the signals and interpret consciously only a few of them at any time. Each bit of information, however, is retained and plays an unconscious part in understanding. Thus, based upon our experiences, we give meanings to the messages we receive; we reconstruct them into information that we can understand on our own terms. These meanings may be appropriate, or they may be misinterpretations resulting from ambiguity or lack of adequate information.

A leafless tree can tell us that the season is fall or winter. The message is present even without our being there to interpret it. This example, though, illustrates the problem of ambiguity. Taken as sufficient to convey the entire message, a bare tree can mislead us. If the other trees are bare, the air is cool, and the ground is covered with snow, we can assume that indeed it is winter. If the grass and the other trees are green, the air is warm, and flowers are blooming, then we must assume that it is spring or summer and that the bare tree is either diseased or dead. We construct the complete message from a combination of details.

Since interpretation is an essential aspect of communication, a good opportunity exists for misunderstanding. To understand any message fully, we must consider both its sender and its receiver. The context of the communicative event is no less important, since we translate contextual details into parts of the message. This process presents the possibility that some messages we receive are not the messages transmitted to us. The sender's implications, our inferences, and ambiguities in the information allow us to misinterpret the communication.[1] Meaning, therefore, is doubly subjective, relying on both the sender and the receiver for parts of its content. Although the result is often confusion, these very stumbling blocks are put to good advantage by groups seeking private means of interaction. Thus gays have capitalized on the subjectivity of interpretation as one way of identifying and communicating with one another without their homosexuality becoming evident to straights.

The degree to which the gay identity is foregrounded varies according to context, as do the functions of gay folklore. The less gay the context, the more likely the folklore is to function primarily for identification and covert communication.

The gay bar communicates a number of messages; its lighting, its layout, and its ambience all contribute to this process. Dim, colored lights convey a sense of privacy and intimacy. The floor plan generally allows the patrons easy visual access to people throughout the bar, but it also requires that, when crowded, patrons must come into close contact with one another. Indeed, the proxemics of the gay bar stand in marked contrast to those of social situations in the mainstream white American culture. Western tradition requires us to maintain a certain distance from one another and provides various coping mechanisms in case we find ourselves caught unavoidably close to someone else; in gay bars (and social situations as well), by contrast, these barriers are removed and closeness is encouraged. As one of the men Edmund White interviewed said, "This place is all about touching. . . . They kept fiddling with the design till they got it right, till everyone had to slip and slide against everyone else."[2] The gay bar makes the statement, "This place is ours; we can be ourselves; we can openly touch and express affection for one another; we can openly seek sexual partners. We can do these things because this place and this time are ours and are subject to our standards rather than straight values."

Other gay contexts include business establishments frequented primarily by homosexual people. Like the bars, these are places where gays can be open about their sexual orientation and can talk freely. Especially in larger cities, for example, there are gay restaurants that offer a safe environment more relaxed than the atmosphere of the bars. There are even entire gay neighborhoods (the "gay ghettos"). Gay social and religious organizations as well as private parties for gays offer additional opportunities for homosexual people to relate to each other *as* homosexual people. Persons present in gay contexts are usually identified by others as gay, regardless of their reasons for being there. Until otherwise informed, most gays tend to assume that all others in such places are homosexually oriented.[3]

Stores, streets, cultural events, office parties, churches, most bars, and indeed most places in our society are nongay contexts in which gays must be careful about how much information they reveal about themselves. These situations require covert communication strategies if homosexual people are to be able to recognize and communicate with one another without being discovered.

Finally, there are semigay contexts like certain parks, streets, and other places where gay people meet, but since these are public places used by many straight people as well, gays must again rely on covert strategies to avoid detection.

The American gay subculture has developed an extensive system of communication.[4] In addition to the argot, members of the community use many subtle (and not so subtle) nonverbal signals to communicate with and relate to other gays. For communication to be effective, rules must be agreed upon; people must know how to convey and interpret information. In the gay subculture there are several strategies employed in communication that are also common to other forms of gay folklore.

One such strategy is humor, which is pervasive in the gay community, a fact reflected in the language, its words, and its usage. The term *TV*, for example, means "transvestite," a simple contraction; but *transvestite*, by extension, is used to mean "television," a funny reversal typical of gay English. Place names frequently make use of such humor. Gay neighborhoods are sometimes given names like *Lavender Hill, Homo Heights, Vaseline Alley*, and *the Swish Alps*.[5] A gay bar in Bloomington is in a building that previously housed the local Moose Lodge; poking fun at the stodginess and conservatism assumed to be endemic among straight people belonging to such organizations, the owners named their bar Bullwinkle's, after the moose in the children's cartoon program. A bar frequented by men who dress in black leather, who often ride motorcycles, and who are generally presumed to prefer sadomasochistic sexual acts is called, naturally enough, a *leather bar*. If some of its patrons tend to be more effeminate than one would generally expect, the bar is referred to as a *patent leather bar*, a term that mocks the intensity associated with those who are part of the leather culture. The humor of these last two examples exhibits the essence of camp—deflating pomposity and underscoring the absurd underlying the serious.[6]

Puns are common in gay conversations. For example, a middle-aged graduate student known to have a preference for teenagers was talking about his studies. He said, "I haven't decided whether to major in American [literature] and minor in British, or major in British and minor in American." Another man said, "Well, Bill, I would have thought you'd major in minors." This type of verbal agility is quite common in the gay subculture. A sharp wit and a sharp tongue are prized possessions. Such word play requires special linguistic competence, a skill that gays develop probably because of the oral nature of the subculture and because of the pervasiveness of humor in the community.[7]

Some terms lend themselves particularly well to puns. *Fairy* and *faggot*, generally used by straights pejoratively, are two of these. Almost any time gays hear the word *fairy* (or the nearly homophonous *ferry*) used in a nongay context they turn it into a pun. S. Steinberg even used the pun in the title of his book *A Fairy Tale*, a story about a gay Jewish man and his matchmaking aunt. "Let's ride the ferry" is an obvious sexual pun. A faggot is not only a gay person; a faggot is a piece of wood to be burned, and the clipped form *fag* can mean "cigarette." *Fagged out* means "tired." *Flaming faggot* is a common phrase that takes on added meaning when someone suggests putting another log on the fire. (*Flaming* means "carrying on in a blatantly effeminate manner," and is probably derived from *flamboyant*.) The humor also has somber overtones since many gays believe that homosexual people were burned at the stake during the Middle Ages. Requesting a fag (almost always done to set up the pun, since *fag* in this sense is obsolete in the United States) may result in a response like, "I want one too!" A man bored and offering his goodbyes in a gay bar, when asked if he is leaving, may respond, "Yes, I'm about fagged out." In doing so he not only says he is tired; he is also commenting on the people in the bar, saying in effect, "I've seen enough of these people. I'm leaving."

Related to puns are double entendres, which are based upon another strategy used in gay communication: ambiguity. The covert nature of many messages is created by sending an ambiguous signal; some key element necessary for a definite interpretation is missing from the communication. Ambiguous signals are used so that the message can be denied if the receiver takes offense when he interprets the information as the sender may have intended originally. The dual nature of the communication allows its originator to claim his intention is innocent and that the receiver has inferred a message that was not sent. At the same time, the gay man's dual cultural membership—gay and straight— provides him with a background from which to make double interpretations.

In the following double entendre, heard in a gay bar in Bloomington, the ambiguity is rather obvious. Feeling his attempt at finding a sexual partner for the evening to be futile, one man said, "Well, I guess I'll go home and do something constructive, like knit." Another man responded, "But you only have one needle." The first man replied, "So I'll crochet." The exchange was spontaneous and the reactions were quick; nothing was laboriously thought out. The humor goes a bit deeper than it first appears, for it plays upon the stereotype of the effeminate gay male. Both knitting and crocheting are consid- ered boring and are associated with women. A man with only one needle (or penis) cannot engage in a cooperative endeavor like knitting, which requires two needles working together. Thus he must make do with the equipment at hand: having but one needle, he must crochet (masturbate). Since this encoun- ter took place between two men, each of whom knew the other was gay, and because it occurred within a gay context, both intended meanings were clear to those who heard the exchange. The two were simply engaging in a bit of word play. Had the men continued the conversation along similar lines, the double entendres could have been used to lay the groundwork for a sexual proposition.

John Reid, in *The Best Little Boy in the World,* gives an example of the type of nonverbal ambiguity gays are accustomed to interpreting.

His . . . apartment sent gay bleeps into my radar, bleeps that would probably not show up on a straight screen, like the tube of K-Y in the

medicine chest or the Barbra Streisand albums among his record collection. I wondered: Could Esquire be gay? I remembered the time we had played handball on his membership at the New York Athletic Club (no blacks and only twelve Jews allowed, but some faggots and lots of closet cases) and what remarkable [*sic*] good shape he was in. I wondered why he had separated from his wife and why they had had no children.[8]

The ambiguous cues were sufficient to alert the narrator that he should watch for additional hints that might confirm his suspicions regarding his friend's orientation.

Ambiguity offers another advantage. A person wishing to ignore one meaning of an ambiguous message can do so simply by taking the signal at its face value. He can in this way avoid a conversation on a topic he wishes not to talk about or resist an attempt to shift the conversation to a more intimate level.[9] The problem with ambiguity is that it can result in misinterpretation when none is intended. A speaker may wish to convey some information secretly to someone else, who misunderstands just as the outsiders do. Thus an ambiguous signal may have to be reinforced with other cues until the intended receiver no longer can have any doubt as to the message.

Inversion is a third strategy common in gay communication. Grace Sims Holt, writing about black English, says that "the phenomenon of inversion is a practical necessity for people in subordinate positions." She goes on to explain that blacks co-opted the white man's language, inverting meanings, taking pride in words whites used pejoratively in describing blacks. The whites were not aware of this word play, so it became a way in which blacks could covertly assert themselves without being punished. The result was the blacks' maintenance of a sense of dignity and group cohesion.[10]

Not only does inversion involve a coding that provides secrecy; it also offers a means of insulting the people who are so adept at stigmatizing gays, a way of expressing contempt that frequently passes unrecognized by those who have been insulted. Inversion also conveys a defiance of heterosexual standards as well. It is a way of saying to straights, "We do not accept your morality. We have our own culture with its own ethics, and these are the rules by which we live." Drag is a highly visible form of nonverbal inversion, and as such exhibits this defiance. Drag is essentially aggressive: gay men present themselves in women's attire, in direct contravention of cultural norms.

Humor, ambiguity, and inversion are often conveyed in gay language through certain paralinguistic features worthy of a detailed study in their own right. As Maurer states in referring to argots, "[they] differ from the standard language in some aspects of structure, and especially in intonation, pitch, and juncture."[11]

Intonation is a feature played with extensively in gay English. As in standard English, many aspects of meaning are conveyed by intonation, sarcasm in particular. And since sarcasm is a form of inversion based primarily on sound rather than denotation, it is especially suited to gay intonation patterns. The word *flawless,* denoting someone who is especially attractive or something extremely well done, is pronounced with heavy emphasis on the first syllable and a falling inflection on the second. *Thank you,* spoken with a rising and then falling inflection, is an interjection expressing emphasis, a sort of oral italics. *For days* is a similar phrase, but it carries with it a sense of great quantity. "Lipstick for days!" means, "She's wearing a really thick layer of lipstick." In other words, it is similar to the English idiom *that just won't quit. Lipstick for days* is spoken beginning at a high tonal level, dropping to a low level for two syllables, and then rising to a medium level on the last syllable.

If we reduce intonation to these three tonal levels—high, medium, and low—we can make basic diagrams of the intonation patterns of these expressions. In the diagram below, dots and lines represent syllables, lines standing for syllables held longer than usual; curved lines indicate syllables beginning at one level and rising or falling to another.

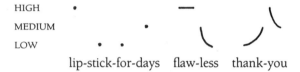

```
HIGH       •              —              \
MEDIUM            •             \    /\
LOW          •  •              \  _/
        lip-stick-for-days   flaw-less   thank-you
```

In contrast to the gay argot, *flawless* and *thank you* in standard English would be rendered more nearly as follows:

```
HIGH
MEDIUM    •          •
LOW           •          •
       flaw-less   thank-you
```

(*Lipstick for days* would not occur in standard English.) This playing with pitch and stress, the exaggeration of tonality, is basic to gay English.

Gays use their argot for secrecy, when relaxing with other gay people, and as a means of preserving and passing on much of their cultural heritage. Just as immigrants generally retain Old World traditions in their native tongues, so do gay people couch a substantial amount of their lore in the gay argot.

Many words in the gay argot are borrowed from the specialized languages of other groups, like prostitutes, drug addicts, and actors.[12] Bruce Rodgers, in *Gay Talk,* offers derivations of many of the 12,000 terms he defines. Among the languages he lists as origins are Chinese, French, Greek, Gullah, Hawaiian, Louisiana Creole, and Yiddish. A large part of the vocabulary, however, is composed of words that gays have created or to which they have applied their own meanings, such as *nelly,* a word used to describe someone who is effeminate (possibly an intensification of *nervous nelly*), and *TV.*[13] The argot is nothing if not eclectic.

A person entering the gay subculture is faced with the problem of acquiring this new language. He learns the argot in many ways. Much of it he absorbs by hearing it used again and again, an osmotic process parallel to the acquisition of one's native tongue. He adds new words to his vocabulary from time to time by asking friends what specific terms mean, and on occasion someone will volunteer information, saying, "Do you know what we call . . . ?" Sometimes the "teacher" will even suggest the reason that *x* is used to mean "y."

Learning occurs in many gay settings, including gay bars, which Evelyn Hooker calls "training and integration centers for the [gay] community." She goes on to say that "once he has 'come out' . . . the process of education proceeds with rapid pace. Eager and willing tutors . . . teach him the special language."[14] After learning the core word stock, the fledgling member of the community may choose to use it. If so, he may begin to use a sprinkling of words here and there, gradually becoming comfortable with the language and fluent in speaking it. At this point he has reached the fifth stage of gay acculturation: serving as a model.

The argot has spread throughout the subculture; its use is not restricted to a given part of the country. Paul H. Gebhard explains how this dissemination is possible:

Because homosexuality cuts across all social and occupational classes its argot is enriched from many sources. A beautifully apt new term can be invented and within a short time be in the mouths of both the underworld and the socially elite. Due to mobility in the United States a standard form of the argot is nationwide, but there appear to be local colloquialisms and special usages.[15]

One type of mobility that is particularly significant in the spread of gay English is travel. Many gays travel extensively, have gay friends throughout the United States, and visit gay communities whenever possible. In doing so, they pass on new terms (and jokes, as well as other traditions) to those they visit, and in turn acquire new material from them that they bring home.

Some parts of the gay argot are as mundane as others are colorful. The following examples offer a sense of the variety the language exhibits.[16]

Active describes a man who takes the inserter role in oral or anal intercourse. He is the person who "gets done" during a sexual act. The "doer," or insertee, is *passive.* For example, a man who *gives head* (fellation) or *rims* (performs anilingus) is passive, and the man being fellated or rimmed is active. Most homosexual acts are of a more mutual nature than this distinction implies. There are some men, however, who are exclusively active or passive, or who at least prefer one role to the other. Oral intercourse is *French* and anal sex is *Greek,* these terms playing upon the stereotypes of the sexual preferences of men from France and Greece. (Edmund White wonders whether "archaeologists in the future [will] speculate about our obsessive interest in foreign verbs—French active, Greek passive.")[17] *Switch-hitters* are bisexual men; since they have sexual relations with both men and women, they are also said to be *AC/DC.* A person who is very masculine in appearance is said to be *butch*; his effeminate counterpart is *fem (femme).* Another term for an effeminate male is *swishy,* which is almost synonymous with *nelly.* (*Swishy* carries a connotation of effeminate movements in addition to voice and mannerisms.) One who is *flaming,* behaving in an exaggeratedly and obviously effeminate way, can also be called *screaming. Flaming* is often used as a modifier for *faggot* (probably because of the puns possible and the alliteration created by combining the terms), and both *flaming* and *screaming* are used in tandem with *queen.*

Queen, ultimately from the Greek *gyne,* "woman" (through Indo-European *gwen-* to Old English *cwene*),[18] is a standard term used by gays in many senses. The word often carries a connotation of effeminacy (read "negative connotation") and all of its attributes: passivity, weakness, perhaps a bit of flamboyance. It is also used quite often as a term of endearment, a sort of affectionate insult. "You tired old queen" is not nearly as derogatory as it sounds. (*Tired* means "used up"—not just sexually—"jaded," "washed up," and so forth, rather than "exhausted"; it means "worn out" in the sense of having succumbed to excessive wear and tear.) Using this phrase is comparable to calling a friend who makes a silly mistake a dummy. *Queen* is used in innumerable compounds. A *drag queen* is a man who likes to go in drag; a *dinge queen* is a white man who prefers black men, and a *snow queen* is a black who prefers Caucasians. A man whose interests lie with Orientals is called a *rice queen*; he is sometimes said to have *yellow fever.*

There are many other gay terms for designating people. *Bitch* is used as both a vocative and a noun; it can, like *queen,* be used either affectionately or pejoratively. *Girl* is a standard word meaning "gay male"; its use is frequently accompanied by feminine pronouns. *Queen, bitch,* and *girl* are good examples of inversion. Another vocative that can be used to express affection is *Miss Thing.* The word *chicken* refers to boys, especially ones not beyond their early teens. A *chicken hawk* is an older man who prefers younger sexual partners. A *troll* is someone who is ugly and often well beyond middle age. An occasional sexual partner or a "one-night stand" is a *trick*; the man with whom one has a continuing relationship is his *lover.* Since homosexual people have been culturally sterilized, being considered to be nonreproductive, gays have adopted the word *breeders* (often occurring in the phrase "filthy breeders") to refer contemptuously to straights. *Clone* has recently been added to the gay vocabulary to designate a particular gay appearance. As White describes him, the

Castro Street Clone . . . [has] a strongly marked mouth and swimming, soulful eyes (the effect of the mustache); a V-shaped torso by metonymy from the open V of the half-unbuttoned shirt above the sweaty chest; rounded buttocks squeezed in jeans, swelling out from the clinched-in waist, further emphasized by the charged erotic insignia of colored handkerchiefs and keys; a crotch instantly accessible through the buttons (bottom one already undone) and enlarged by being pressed, along with the scrotum, to one side; legs molded in perfect, powerful detail; the feet simplified, brutalized and magnified by the boots.[19]

Lesbians, especially ones who are stereotypically butch to the point of being hypermasculine, are called *dykes, bull dykes,* and *diesel dykes.* Women, straight ones in particular, are given the extremely derogatory label *fish,* derived from the similarity of vaginal odors to those of fish. By extension, a Jewish woman is *gefilte fish.* One who is a woman by sex (as opposed to a drag queen or female impersonator) is *real,* or an *RG (real girl).* If she spends a great deal of time in the presence of gay men, she is called a *fag hag* or *fruit fly,* both derogatory terms and both based upon insulting epithets for gay men.

Some of these gay terms have entered standard English; *coming out* and *closet* are the most common ones to have done so. Almost everyone uses these words now, because—like many gay terms—they are especially apt for conveying certain ideas. *Closet queens* (or *closeted people*), though, fearful of being discovered, generally still refrain from using them. The majority of the vocabulary, however, is still restricted to gay usage. A good example is *tearoom,* a public restroom where homosexual encounters take place—often anonymously through a *glory hole,* an opening gouged through the partition between two toilets. Large women's shoes are sometimes called *Joan Crawford come-fuck-me pumps* (or *Joan Crawford ankle-strapped open-toed fuck me's*). The phrase is often used in referring to a drag queen's shoes, and sometimes is applied to men's footwear as well. A person who is fussy about appearances and behavior almost to the point of being prissy is *piss-elegant* or *chichi* (from the French *chic*). Piss-elegance is pseudo-elegance, a dimestore version of true luxury and taste. To *dish* is to gossip, and to *read* (or *read* [someone's] *beads*) involves really chewing someone out. (*Read* is probably derived from *read the riot act to.*) A person might get read for *working deceit,* playing nasty (rather than harmless) tricks on another person, such as sabotaging a female impersonator's gown before her performance. Beads can be dropped as well as read. To *drop beads* is to drop hints about one's homosexuality. To keep from dropping beads gay people often try to avoid masculine and feminine pronouns in referring to their close friends; instead they will use various convolutions like "a friend of mine and I," "someone I know from school," and "this person I met."

As with language itself, humor can be used to elicit information from others about themselves. By telling jokes on sexual topics, for example, a narrator may obtain details about his listener's orientation from his response.[20] The response to a racist or a misogynistic anecdote can shed light on the listener's attitudes toward women and toward racial groups other than his own. The information received about a person in this way can be used to identify him as gay, or as a bigot, or as a misogynist. Of course the identification must remain tentative, for as with a leafless tree, much more must be communicated before a definite determination can be made.

Using humor as a communicative device offers certain advantages over conversation. One of the values of humor lies in its usefulness in facilitating interaction.[21] It offers us a means of quickly bringing a conversation to an intimate level, avoiding introductions and small talk. And, as John Herrick puts it, "Jokes are an easy way to win favor."[22] Humor gives our listeners insight into our personalities and their responses inform us about them. Since humor is supposedly not serious, messages that might otherwise cause offense can be couched within jokes or other forms of humorous expression. In this way, a listener is allowed to ignore the message if he finds it offensive. Should he be interested in the underlying statement, however, he is encouraged to continue the interaction, which he will generally enter through humor himself.

Regardless of our attitudes toward it, humor is a very serious medium indeed. Joking with an unfamiliar person is a delicate process, because it is an easy matter to violate the bounds of propriety if one is unfamiliar with his listener's values. Humor allows us to express ideas that are normally socially inexpressible, and in doing so we give our listeners quite a bit of insight into our thoughts and values.[23]

To function as secret communication among gays, jokes must contain a highly esoteric referent. Recognition of the humor suggests that the listener is probably homosexual. If the joke relies on ambiguity, with its humor making sense on both levels, the clue provided by the response is less definite; the secrecy of the communication is more secure, however, since the other members of the audience will probably find the joke funny too and will not be likely to ask for an explanation. Within these guidelines, humor can be employed to imply one's own homosexuality as well as to say that the narrator suspects that his listener may be gay. In exploring someone's sexual orientation through joking, one might also use humor to introduce or conceal a proposition.

The following examples illustrate some of the messages implicit in the humor of gay men.

A Greek, an Italian, and a Jew were walking down the beach and found a lamp. They picked it up and rubbed it, and a genie came out and said, "I'm going to grant you each a wish, but there's one condition: you can't do anything ethnic for twenty-four hours. If you do you'll vanish."

So they were walking down the street and passed a restaurant. They could smell the spaghetti, and the lasagna, and all the pasta, and the Italian said, "I'm hungry. I'm going to go in and have something to eat." And the Greek and the Jew said, "No! You can't do that! That's ethnic!" And he said, "Oh, that's ridiculous; everybody's got to eat." So he went in. And just as he stepped through the door—poof!—he vanished.

So the Greek and the Jew went on down the street, and they saw a five-dollar bill lying on the sidewalk. And the Jew said, "Look! Somebody dropped some money. I'm going to pick it up." And the Greek said, "No, you can't do that! That's ethnic!" And the Jew said, "Nonsense. Everybody needs money." And he bent over to pick up the five-dollar bill and—poof!—they both vanished.

This joke draws its humor from a number of stereotypes: the Italian's fondness of pasta, the Jew's thriftiness (or even miserliness), and the Greek's predilection for anal intercourse. Thus it communicates a slightly negative attitude toward these ethnic groups. The implied pedication of the Jew by the Greek is too esoteric a reference for most straights to understand. By telling this joke the narrator was saying, in effect, "I'm gay (as you can tell, since I understand this joke), and I think you may be gay too." If the listener understood the joke and laughed, the narrator would have been encouraged to explore the matter further.

Two gay men were riding down the street in a taxi, and one said, "I've got to fart." And the other one said, "Well, just roll down the window and stick your ass out and fart." So he rolled down the window and stuck out his ass and—"ffff"—he farted. Well, in a few minutes the second one said, "Now *I've* got to fart." So the other one said, "Well, roll down the window, stick your ass out, and fart." So he rolled down the window, stuck out his ass, and—"ffff"—he farted.
Well, they went on down the road and in a little while the cab driver said, "I've got to fart." So one of the gays said, "Well, roll down the window, stick out your ass, and fart. I'll hold the wheel for you." So the gay man reached over the seat, took the wheel, and the driver rolled down the window, stuck out his ass, and—
"bbbrrraackkk"—he farted. And the first gay man turned to the second one and said, "See, I *told* you he was a virgin."

Tallulah Bankhead was having dinner in a restaurant in San Francisco, and there were these two gay men there who were really excited about having dinner in the same restaurant as Tallulah. Tallulah had to go past their table on the way to the restroom, so they decided to ask her a question so they could talk with her. One of them said, "Excuse me, Miss Bankhead, but we're having a discussion, and we wondered which is better, Kipling or Browning?" And she said, "Why, dahling, I wouldn't know. I've never kipled."[24]

Both of these jokes rely on esoteric referents for their humor as does the ethnic joke above. The story about the taxi driver might be understood by straight listeners to be about anal intercourse. (Had the driver not been a "virgin," his flatulence supposedly would have produced a hiss, since his anal sphincter would have been looser.) But to a heterosexual audience the Tallulah Bankhead joke would make no sense at all. It might seem mildly funny that Tallulah took *Browning* and *Kipling* to be gerunds and responded by turning *Kipling* into a verb, but the humor lies in the fact that *browning is* a gerund. By pretending to take the authors' names as verb forms, Tallulah has at once indicated that she is well acquainted with gay life and that she has no time for useless conversations with fawning admirers. These two jokes, like the previous one, imply the teller's homosexuality and serve as exploratory devices.

The next few joking questions, through their homoerotic references, function in the same way when told by one man to another.

Did you hear about the original hard-luck guy?
He crossed a bloodsucker with a cockroach and got a bloodroach.

What do you get if you cross a rooster with an M&M?
A cock that comes in your mouth and not in your hand.

What do you get when you cross a rooster and an owl?
A cock that stays up all night.

What do you get when you cross a rooster and a jar of peanut butter?
A cock that sticks to the roof of your mouth.

What do you get if you cross a rooster and a telephone pole?
A forty-five-foot cock that wants to reach out and touch someone.[25]

Do you know how to get four gay men on a barstool?
Turn it upside-down.

What's better than sixty-nine?
Seventy-seven, because it's eight more [ate more].

Did you hear about the woman who walked into the sperm bank?
She said, "Ah ahnna ake uh uhahsit." ["I want to make a deposit," spoken as though the mouth is full.]

If the listener expresses an appreciation of these jokes, then the teller (if he is interested sexually in his audience) may proceed with his exploration. Eventually he may make an outright proposition if his preliminary endeavors seem to have been successful.

In the late 1970s an anatomically correct male doll was being sold for homosexual men. "Gay Bob" came with his own closet, and one of his hands was designed so that he could hold his penis. Very soon after sales of the doll started, a joke began to circulate:

What do you get when you put two Gay Bob dolls together?
Oral Roberts.

By spring 1981 this joke had lost its topical reference:

What do you get when you put two gay men named Bob together?
Oral Roberts.

The joke still contains the open disdain many gays express for religion, particularly for the type espoused by conservative ministers such as Roberts. It is still rather funny. But because the Gay Bob dolls are not widely known outside the gay community, the loss of that reference has made the joke less valuable as an exploratory device when told in a nongay context.

Through the pun made in the following joke an intimacy is expressed that can also function as an exploratory statement.

Two German men are talking, and one says, "Köln ist ein drechiges Loch." And the other one says, "Ja, aber du sollst mal Mainz sehen." ("Cologne is a shitty hole." "Yes, but you should see Mainz.")

The familiar pronoun *du* underscores the intimacy inherent in the statement *"Du sollst mal Mainz sehen,"* in which the elision between *Mainz* and *sehen* makes the phrase homophonous with *"Du sollst mal mein sehen"* ("You should see mine").

Prejudices can also be communicated through jokes. The bias against people of Polish background is common in American humor, as are racism and misogyny. This fact is no less true among gay men, as the following examples illustrate.

> How many niggers does it take to blacktop a driveway?
> Only two, if you spread them real thin.

> Why do women have legs?
> Because if they didn't, they'd leave sticky trails like slugs.

Frequently various messages of this sort are combined in a single joke.

> Did you hear about the Polack who sucked his first cock?
> He got a mouthful of feathers.

This joke brings together the anti-Polish prejudice, expressed in the Pole's stereotypical stupidity (sucking a rooster instead of a penis), and the listener's inference that the joke is about oral sex. Of course the listener is bound to fall into the trap, but as with many of the jokes discussed above, the quality and nature of his response—positive or negative—sends a message about his awareness, and thus possibly about his orientation, to his narrator.

By providing a means of covert communication, a way of conveying potentially offensive messages, and expressing ideas common to members of the subculture, humor serves as a very useful extension of language.

The same is true of personal experience narratives. Although such stories function most strongly as cohesive mechanisms, they do convey messages and attitudes. For example, Michael Monroe tells the following story to "people who are talking about whether or not they should tell their parents or [who ask] how your parents reacted to finding out you were gay." He goes on to point out that "it's an offensive story, looking back. It was a very rude thing to do to my parents. But having done it, I feel I might as well share the knowledge."

> The one I tell most often is in terms of the very gradual process that I had of coming out to my parents, whereby I came home from my first semester at school, ready and armed with my new gay lingo and gestures and that sort of thing—which my parents wouldn't have identified as being gay; they just would have thought it was weird.
> But then I came home for Thanksgiving maybe, one year, and picked up a trick at the bar the night before. And he was from Dayton, so we couldn't go to his house. And I thought, "Well, it's three o'clock in the morning; surely my family will all be asleep, and [we can] go upstairs and nobody will know the difference." And I got home with him at three o'clock in the morning and *everyone* was still awake. My father was out in the garage working on his car, and my mother I guess was basting the

turkey; my sister was helping my father, and my brother was—I don't know—wandering around.

And so I tried to go in the upstairs way, which would have avoided all the traffic, and I couldn't get in. The door was locked, so I had to go right through the house. And I met my brother on the stairs and he kind of gave me a funny look, like—I assumed he figured out what was going on; he didn't say anything.

But he spent the night, and in the morning I awoke to the sound of bustling around, people getting ready to go to the Thanksgiving service at church. And every time somebody ascended the staircase my heart was in my throat, with no lock on the door. And for reasons only *she* can tell you, my mother did *not* come bursting into the room. She knocked meekly on the door and said, "Michael, wake up. We're having breakfast in half an hour and we expect you to go to church with us." So I got up, and my friend got up and dressed, and I sent him out the upstairs way and he drove off, and I went down. And as I was *just* settling myself in my seat at the dining table, my mother said, "Isn't your friend staying for breakfast?"

I thought, *"Well, she's* being calm." And I stuttered and said something about, "Well, he has to be back home in a hurry." And no more was said until the end of the meal, when my mother said, "Well now, we're having lots of guests for lunch, so I want you all to come right home from church and clean up your rooms, and clean up your bathrooms, and Michael, clean up wherever your friend stayed." He obviously had stayed with me, and I believe the door to the guest room was open, so it was apparent that he hadn't stayed there.

That night I had the audacity to ask for the car again, to go out again. And my father went through his usual song and dance about, "But it's eleven o'clock at night"—you know—"where are you going at eleven o'clock at night that—you should be coming home, not going out at this hour." And I went through *my* usual song and dance about how my friends keep late hours. And then he said, "Well, okay, you can borrow the car, but sometime we need to talk about last night."

Well, he was there working on his car with my sister and her boyfriend, so I said sure, assuming that he would choose some more appropriate moment. But he just kind of plowed ahead and said, "Well, where did your friend stay?"

And I said, "Well, upstairs."

"Where upstairs?"

"In my room."

"On the *floor*?" he asked.

So I took a deep breath and said, "In my bed"—which *is* a twin bed, it's not terribly large. And he seemed at that point quite taken aback—I mean he *really* had his head in the sand—and kind of choked. I think by this time my sister and her boyfriend had both stopped working on the car and were watching with interest.

And he kind of choked and said, "Well, we have plenty of beds in this house. I don't think it's necessary for you to double up. Please don't ever do that again. Now take the car and go."

And that was as much as we'd ever discussed about my life-style, my coming out. At that point I felt—well, I had no intention of bringing up the subject because I knew that—and that proved that they were—had no interest in hearing about it. They weren't going to be prepared for it. It wasn't going to be a valuable communication. So I left it like that.[26]

In that narrative Michael vividly tells his audience how his parents learned he was gay, how he dealt with their discovery by trying to avoid mentioning it, and how his parents reacted. Despite the rudeness of his actions, Michael's parents tacitly agree to accept his homosexuality as long as they are not confronted with it. Michael's message to his audience is, "I've been through letting my parents know. This is how it happened, and although it was awkward and done in a less-than-tactful way, I came through the situation successfully. My family still loves me. I did it, and so can you if you need to." Thus we see that narratives, like jokes, carry both implicit and explicit messages.

In addition to specialized language, jokes, narratives, and other aspects of verbal folklore, nonverbal cues are also used in recognition. Many gay people claim an ability to recognize other gays on sight. Very few, however, can explain how this talent operates. One of my informants says that it is "a second sense. The majority of the time I've been right. . . . [It's] something that's born within you, something that you have no power over."[27] John Herrick gave a similar response: "Why, it's my feminine intuition," a typical gay statement employing humor that plays on the stereotype of the effeminate gay male. He then listed some of the cues that suggest a man is gay. A homosexual man who does not want to be identified as gay overcompensates, acting a bit more masculine than a heterosexual man; he stands more erectly; he has a firmer handshake. A gay man's appearance has a "finer polish" than that of a straight man, and as a gay man he will hold another man's gaze longer than a heterosexual male will.[28]

Nonverbal cues are learned in much the same way as verbal ones—through observation, asking, and being told—and gays are adept at their use. Joseph J. Hayes maintains that

gays are more sophisticated [than straights] in [using nonverbal communication], depend on it more, and know better how to manipulate it for their own ends. Moreover, their necessary involvement in role-awareness and role-playing makes them aware of [what a small amount of] important communication is actually put into words. Sophistication in nonverbal language also makes gays aware of the dangers that lurk everywhere in the use of spoken language.[29]

Drawing upon this ability, gays take note of many cues emitted by other men through their behavior, their clothing, and their jewelry and other accessories.

The range of nonverbal signals the subculture has created aids in maintaining a double identity, remaining invisible to straights and yet recognizable to other gays.[30] Some of the cues are becoming more widely recognized outside the subculture, such as the lambda and the inverted pink triangle, two of the major symbols of the gay liberation movement; both are sometimes worn as buttons, and the lambda is often worn on a necklace or used as a tie-tack.

The lowercase Greek letter λ carries several meanings. First of all, it represents scales, and thus balance. The Greeks considered balance to be the constant adjustment necessary to keep opposing forces from overcoming each other. The hook at the bottom of the right leg of the lambda represents the action required to reach and maintain balance. To the Spartans the lambda meant unity. They felt that society should never infringe on anyone's individuality and freedom. The Romans adopted the letter to represent "the light of knowledge shed into the darkness of ignorance." Finally, in physics the symbol designates an energy exchange.[31] Thus the lambda, with all its meanings, is an especially apt symbol for the gay liberation movement, which energetically seeks a balance in society and which strives through enlightenment to secure equal rights for homosexual people.

By contrast, in an unusual form of inversion, many gays have begun wearing inverted pink triangles (often with the slogan "Never again!" or in circles with diagonal lines through them) as a reminder of the oppression to which gays are still subjected. During the Holocaust the Nazis sent many non-Jews to the concentration camps, including gypsies, religious dissidents, and homosexual men and women. Untold tens of thousands of homosexual people were forced to wear the pink triangle and, like millions of Jews, were ultimately exterminated.[32]

Other visual cues are in evidence outside specifically gay contexts. Jewelry of various types functions as an identifying mark. Men's necklaces, for example, were for a long time indicators of a homosexual orientation. In the 1960s, however, members of the counterculture (and later straight men in general) co-opted this signal, decreasing its value by confusing its message.[33] The same process affected the meaning of a single earring worn by a man; although it is still an indicator of homosexuality, remnants of the drug culture, fans of punk rock music, and more recently many college students and other types of men have had their ears pierced. The "pinky ring," a ring worn on the little finger, is a third ambiguous signal. For many years gay men have used the pinky ring to signify their orientation, but as more and more straight people have begun wearing these rings, their level of ambiguity has risen greatly. Men involved in the arts often wear pinky rings with no intention of suggesting a homosexual preference. Recently some gay men have begun wearing rings on their middle fingers (and occasionally on their forefingers), but again, these signals are somewhat confused, since a few straight men wear their wedding bands on the middle fingers of their left hands.

Many gay signals are given added meaning by their placement. The left side of the body signifies active, the right side passive. Thus a pinky ring on the left hand or an earring in the left ear may indicate that the wearer prefers to take an active or dominant role in sex. Keys worn on the belt or dangling from the pocket provide the same general information.

The most specific messages are conveyed by bandanas. Again the right-left distinction is important, whether the handkerchief is carried in the back pockets or worn around the arms, wrists, or legs. When worn around the neck or as a headband the bandana indicates that the wearer is willing to take either role. The multiplicity of colors provides additional information. Although there is some variation in interpretation, there is generally a common understanding of each color's meaning. A white bandana represents a desire for masturbation; a man wearing it on the left wants to be masturbated, and one wearing it on the right is willing to perform this act for his partner as well as for himself. Light blue (robin's egg) is the color for oral intercourse, and dark blue (navy) stands for anal intercourse. A man wearing a black bandana is interested in sadomasochism. Red designates fistfucking (brachioproctic intercourse). A hustler (male prostitute) wears a green bandana on his left; a man seeking a hustler's services wears a similar handkerchief on the right. Olive green expresses an interest in military uniforms. A mustard colored bandana, worn on the left, means that the wearer is "well hung," having a penis at least eight inches long when erect; the same bandana worn on the right means that the wearer is seeking someone of such proportions. Yellow stands for watersports, wherein one partner urinates on the other, and brown is worn by those interested in scatological acts. Someone willing to do anything at any time displays an orange bandana on his left. On the right the bandana for some carries the same meaning; for others it is a statement that they are not interested in having sexual relations for the time being.[34] Another item one occasionally sees gay men carrying in their hip pockets is a teddy bear about six inches tall. The teddy bear signals a desire to cuddle or be cuddled.

Black leather is worn by a number of gay men to express a preference for sadomasochism. Charcoal brown leather indicates a neophyte's interest in exploring S&M. Other accoutrements carrying similar meanings include chains, handcuffs (used in particular by men who enjoy B&D—bondage and discipline), and studded leather armbands, belts, and gloves.

Kenneth E. Read asserts that keys and bandanas are fads that change constantly and are not widespread.[35] Although the teddy bear may be a mere fad, the other nonverbal cues discussed above are too tenacious to be considered faddish. They become fads when, in the manner of radical chic, they are adopted by straights. They are also extremely widespread.

Another type of nonverbal communication is drag. Although most aspects of female impersonation function primarily to maintain cohesion and to aid in coping with (as well as expressing) conflict, doing drag does communicate. It can be a statement like, "I am gay, and proud of it. I can be a better woman than a real woman." In this way drag is aggressive, flouting the values of heterosexual culture by flaunting homosexuality. By inverting the meaning of the stereotype, drag imbues with pride a practice generally held in contempt. Female impersonation can, by the same method, also communicate the feminine aspects of a man's personality; it allows him to say, "I have feminine and masculine traits, and I see nothing wrong in expressing both."

Two of the most obvious nonverbal signals used by gays involve eye contact and proxemics. Among gay men, slightly sustained eye contact within a gay context indicates potential sexual interest. It may be followed (after some time) by smiles, nods, an introduction, an offer to buy a drink, an invitation to dance, or some other means of intensifying the encounter. This process is called *cruising*. When similar eye contact occurs in a nongay environment it serves as a means of recognition. Depending on the situation it may lead to cruising.[36]

One also notices among gay men an abandonment of personal space, that invisible shell we all carry around our bodies. No one is normally allowed within this area, but among gay people there is a lot of physical contact, both affectionate and sexual. This violation of personal space is more than a result of people's finding themselves in a crowded room; it is a response to the isolation homosexual people feel in heterosexual society. Everyone needs acceptance and close friends; one way the gay subculture meets this need is by eliminating the barriers normally associated with personal space.[37]

Active use of gay communication strategies is not required for acculturation. Observation of the system in action, however, begins when the gay person reaches level three of acculturation—his first association with the subculture— since at this point he inevitably becomes a passive bearer of these traditions. In addition, since much of the nonverbal communication occurs on a subconscious level, he will almost surely become an active bearer of at least this aspect of gay communication, using some of it—without his awareness—to identify others and to let them know of his orientation. If he reaches level four and begins to practice his new knowledge consciously, then the fifth stage, that of serving as a model for other newcomers, is almost sure to follow.

If gay communication did not meet the needs of the gay subculture, it would not exist. It functions in several ways, helping to define the subculture, marking both members and nonmembers; it is a medium through which the cultural heritage of the gay community can be conveyed; it is a casual, humorous way of communicating with people with whom one feels comfortable; it is a means of discussing taboo subjects openly (or semiopenly) without fear of discovery. And as David Sonenschein suggests, it is a way in which the subculture can give the gay experience meaning.[38] All of these functions of the gay argot are subsumed under one larger role the language plays: it aids in establishing and maintaining subcultural cohesion.

༄ 3

There's No Version like Perversion

COHESION WITHIN THE GAY SUBCULTURE

COHESION IS A very strong need felt by many people; it is a desire for a sense of belonging, a means of relating to others based on a sense of commonality that results in a sense of group identity. Before cohesion can develop, one must be able to identify those with whom one has something in common and to communicate with them to ensure that there is indeed a basis for some sort of relationship to proceed. Homosexuality provides an instant basis for this interaction, even though people may have nothing else in common, since being gay is a stigmatized identity and as such is generally an intimate secret shared only with one's closest friends. Therefore gay people feel a heightened need for cohesion. The gay argot, as we have seen, is one medium through which esoteric communication can take place. For gays the language is both shared and secret, its covert nature enhancing the sense of sharing and intimacy. In this way gay English serves to foster cohesion.

Other aspects of gay folklore are also grounded in shared and secret knowledge. For this reason much of the material is nonsensical to outsiders, thus helping to define the in-group. These esoteric traditions, by inverting stereotypes, flouting the values espoused by the dominant heterosexual culture, allaying fears, and asserting the essential normalcy of gay people, both create and help to maintain cohesion within the subculture.

Humor is one of the most obvious folkloric forms used by people to preserve a sense of group. Gay humor is no exception. Not only do jokes, anecdotes, and other forms of humor function as entertainment; they also are used as attention-getting devices; they serve to lighten the burdens of day-to-day life and oppression; and they make such statements as, "We're all in this together," "We're not so bad after all," "We share something others cannot understand," and "We can have the upper hand, since straights don't know what we're talking about." As Freud states, "A [hostile] joke will allow us to exploit something ridiculous in our enemy which we could not, on account of obstacles in the way, bring forward openly or consciously."[1]

Some jokes, functioning primarily as entertainment, are basically silly little narratives or sets of questions and answers, as are the following examples.

Two gay men are talking, and one says, "I'm pregnant."
The other one says, "Well, at least you know who the father is, don't you?"
And he says, "What? You think I got eyes in the back of my head?"[2]

What do you call a homosexual pygmy?
[Teller holds hand about two feet off the floor.] A little sucker about that high.

What did the elephant say to the naked man?
How do you breathe through that thing?[3]

Who was the Roman who drove a pink chariot?
Ben Gay.[4]

What do elephants and milk have in common?
They both come in quarts.

Why is the Jolly Green Giant strange?
Because he comes in cans.

What do you call a bouncer in a gay bar?
A flame thrower.

Humorous items such as these can put people at ease, helping them forget the problems and conflicts facing them in their careers and in other aspects of their lives. They are safe and understood within the subculture, and thus aid in uniting the members of the community. At the same time these jokes carry significant messages. The first plays with the common stereotype that anal intercourse is the predominant sexual activity among gay men; by contrast, the second joke assumes that oral intercourse is predominant. The third, comparing the penis with an elephant's trunk, alludes to the commonly held notion that men (not just gay men) are obsessed with penis size. The presumed effeminacy of gay men (and their arrested development?) is the topic of the fourth joke, since pink is associated with baby girls; this joke also carries an implied pun—Ben Hur/been her. The next two jokes are puns referring to ejaculation and reflect the current preoccupation of both gay and straight men with sex. All of these jokes could be told by people of either orientation, but several of them would likely cause offense if told to gays by straights, especially the final joke above. The use of the word *flame* makes clear the allusion to the stereotype of gays as flaming queens. When told by gay people, however, this joke carries the message, "We can laugh at the stereotype," thereby functioning as a cohesive force against derision by the straight world. Although not offensive if told by outsiders, the following frequently heard comments that serve to lighten conversation also underscore the sense of cohesion among gays.

"Do you smoke after sex?"
"I don't know; I never looked."

"My mother made me a homosexual."
"If I get her the yarn will she make me one too?"[5]

When used by gay men the "smoking after sex" line, while referring to the common practice of having a cigarette after a sexual encounter, also suggests that gay sexuality must be extremely passionate if it has the potential to leave one smoking. The other comment takes the Freudian theory of distant father–dominant or close-binding mother as a contributor to homosexuality and inverts it, stating that homosexuality is both good and desirable. Thus we see that although many jokes are—on the surface—little more than silliness, it is a silliness that often belies the complexity of the messages the jokes carry on other levels. The following joke is a good example.

You hear about the three faggots that are talking? She says, "If I could become something I would like to become a telephone." The other ones say, "A telephone? What for?" He says, "Imagine, everyone putting their hole, their finger in the hole all day long." So the other one says, "Oh, that's O.K., but I would like to become a dresser's drawer." He says, "A drawer? What for?" He says, "Imagine all those dirty socks and those shorts. Men, nothing but men's smell." The other one says, "That's good, but if I can become something it would be an ambulance." "An ambulance?" "Imagine, them open your rear end, throw the whole body in and going down the street screaming with a big ruby on your head." [All sic.][6]

This joke at first seems to be a bit of fluff poking fun at stereotypical queens who have no higher aims than fulfillment of sexual fantasies. But the real message, much more serious than the humor conveys, is a plea for freedom. Playing on the stereotypes of gays as effeminate, screaming faggots interested in nothing but sex, the joke expresses a desire for tolerance if not acceptance: "Let us be who we are." Beyond that, it also offers veiled promises and threats: "If you give us our freedom, some of us will stay home (like telephones and dressers), minding our own business. Others of us will really flaunt our sexuality; we'll carry your stereotypes of us to extremes and parade them in the streets. We are as diverse in nature as any other group." By providing a forum for expressing concerns and attitudes, veiled in humor though they may be, this joke serves a cohesive function.

Another example is the following version of "The Three Little Pigs."

Once upon a time, in a far off kingdom, there were three pigs. . . . Now the first pig was a square pig. He was so square he thought *I* [the narrator, a female impersonator] was real . . . well so did I, for a long time. . . .

And the second pig was a musician pig, so he was hep; and the third pig was a . . . she was, well (*exaggerated faggot intonation and slight lisp on "she"*) you know, everybody called her "Sissy Pork," you know. (*Laughs.*) God, talk about a nellie pig. (*Laughs.*) And they all thought they'd build themselves some houses. Now the first pig, the square pig, he built his out of bricks and mortar. And the hep pig, the musician pig, he built his out of scotch tape and red lights—oh it was a crazy pad, jug of wine, and a loaf of bread, and (*makes sound of intake of breath*) "Oh mother, you laid a roach on me" (*this said in deep Louis Armstrong voice*).

Sissy Pork (*high voice*) she built hers out of crepe paper, and sequins (*laughs*) and she had a mirrored bedroom, much-used lace curtains (*much laughter*) . . . why is it the girls always understand that and the boys never do? In other words, she done it up brown. Now we're back to the boys again. . . .

Well, anyway, just like advertised, here come the wolf down the highway. He just simply by-passed the square's place all together, went right over to the hep pig's pad, knocked on the door. The pig said (*deep Armstrong voice*), "Like who calls?" The wolf said, "How do you get to Carnegie Hall?" The pig said, "Practice, dad, practice." He said, "Don't stand on that bag of bagels man. Come on in and listen to a little bit of Brubeck." The wolf said, "I'm gonna eat you." He said, "Cool it dad, I don't go that route. . . . Tell you what though (*voice indicates that musician pig is speaking*), you make it about a half a mile down the road, you come across my little gay brother, and he digs a party the most." And with that (*voice higher*) he turned the stereo so loud, it shook the wolf.

He took off down the highway, a half mile . . . and there she was, a-waitin', Sissy Pork (*last two words "faggot" pronunciation*). She had a marcel in her cork-screw tail, spoon-heeled shoes . . . he said, "I'm the big bad wolf." She said (*he imitates the pig's coy stance while replying*), "Why aren't you huffin' and puffin', baby?" (*Laughs.*) He said, "I'm gonna eat you." She said, "Wouldn't you know it . . . (*disgusted look*). (*Audience cracks up.*) Well, God damn it, don't stand in the door, I've got neighbors!" She took him back there to the mirrored bedroom, she started to close the door, she poked her head out . . . she said, "That's the way it goes, girls. Yesterday's wolf is today's sister." [All *sic*.][7]

This story, although told with humor, carries two very strong messages: homosexual people are everywhere (in sets of siblings, in neighborhoods, in "fairy tales," and in "real life"), and not all gays are effeminate. (Sissy Pork may be stereotypical, but the wolf is a strong masculine figure, who in *this* story happens to be gay.)

Other jokes may seem to be insulting (or at least offensive) to both teller and audience when in actuality they are quite popular. This paradoxical situation is a result of what A. R. Radcliffe-Brown calls a joking relationship, which allows participants to tease and even insult each other without being offended.[8]

For example, two gay men could exchange a series of jokes like the following, whereas the same jokes told by straights to gays would usually cause offense.

How many gay men does it take to change a lightbulb?
Two: one to buy the art deco bulb and one to say, "Oh, it's marvelous!"

How many queens does it take to change a lightbulb?
Four: one to change the bulb, two to hold the ladder, and one to say, "Oh, how *nice*."

How many fags does it take to change a lightbulb?
[When the listener indicates that he doesn't know, the teller says:] Oh, you haven't gotten yours changed yet either.

How many gay men does it take to change a lightbulb?
Sixteen: one to put in the bulb, two to hold the ladder, three to give directions, four to decide whether or not it's going in the right place, and six to debate if it's politically correct.

A joking relationship can obtain among gays much more easily than between gays and straights. Homosexual men, therefore, can play with the stereotypes of gays as effeminate (in terms of taste: art deco; speech patterns: *"Oh, it's marvelous!"*; and independence: inability to change a lightbulb) and can make such jokes about themselves. They can also make fun of their overly serious brothers (who in politicizing homosexuality would debate whether something were "politically correct" for the subculture). An outsider, not having the privileges allowed by the joking relationship, would usually receive only animosity were he to tell the same jokes among gays.

The joking relationship also allows a teller to entertain his listeners at the expense of at least one member of the audience, a person who, as Radcliffe-Brown points out, "is required to take no offense." For example, during one joke-telling session I was included as an actor in two jokes, and was made the butt of one of them.

Joe entered a dirty limerick contest. He sent in his three dirtiest limericks and knew that he would win, because he had every dirty limerick ever collected. So a few days later he got back a letter saying, "Congratulations, Mr. Goodwin, you have won second and third prizes in our dirty limerick contest."
"Well," he thought, "This can't be. There must be a mistake. I have every dirty limerick ever written, and I sent in the three dirtiest ones." So he called the sponsor and said, "This is Joe Goodwin. I . . . ."
And the woman said, "Oh, yes, we know who you are, Mr. Goodwin. Congratulations on winning second and third places in our contest."
And he said, "That's what I'm calling about. There must be a mistake. I have every dirty limerick ever written."
And the woman said, "Well, there was one entry sent in by [a radio announcer from a local station] that was dirtier than yours."

So Joe said, "Well, could you read it to me?"

And she said—she was a nice little old lady—so she said, "No, I don't think I could do that."

And he said, "How about if you read it to me, but leave out all the dirty words?"

So she said, "Well, I guess that would be all right. This is the winning limerick:

Da da da da da da da da,
Da da da da da da da da;
Da da da da da,
Da da da da da,
Da da da da da da da fuck!"

Bob died and went to hell, and the devil was showing him around and he saw all these clocks on the wall. The walls were just lined with clocks, and each clock had a name on it. And Bob said, "What are all these clocks for?"

And the devil said, "Well, every time someone plays with himself, the hands go forward an hour."

So Bob said, "Well, where is Joe's clock?"

And the devil said, "Oh, it's in the office; we're using it as a fan."

In these jokes, as in the lightbulb jokes, cohesion is expressed in the form of permitted disrespect, a phenomenon that is a marker, orally reinforcing the feeling of group that exists among the members of the audience. Sharing such seemingly offensive jokes allows the members of the in-group to say, through the joking relationship, "Our group is so cohesive that it can withstand strong insults among its members."

Another cohesive function of jokes is to provide scenarios in which the in-group triumphs over the out-group. The following joke, for example, seems innocent enough:

How many psychiatrists does it take to change a lightbulb?
Only one, but the lightbulb really has to want to change.

The joke is based on the stereotype that homosexual people are mentally ill and in need of professional help, and that psychiatrists can "change" them, making them heterosexual. But the punchline carries the subject further, making the point that psychiatrists cannot "change" gay people, that gays are in control of their lives. The joke thus gives gays the upper hand. It also implies that gays do not *want* to change. Expressing the attitude "gay is good" (or even "gay is better"), this joke offers a psychological victory over oppression.

A similar psychological victory is scored in the next joke.

Jesse James was gonna rob the train, you know. So he got on the train an' uh he says, "Before I do anything I'm gonna tell you people exactly what I'm gonna do. I'm gonna rape all you men and rob all you women."

And some guy stood up and he goes, "Don't you have that in reverse Jesse? Don't you mean you're gonna rape all the women and rob all the men?" And some little fag way in the back says, (*black accent*) "You let Jesse do what she wants to do."[9]

The "little fag way in the back," unlike the other passengers, is in a situation with potential for pleasure. The women will be robbed and the straight men raped, but the "little fag" will have what he presumes will be an enjoyable sexual encounter.

On occasion a joke presents an obvious physical triumph, as in the next example.

There are two guys at the bar, and one is straight and one is gay. And the gay guy says to the straight guy, "Well, have you heard about this new game? It's called barroom football."

And the straight guy says, "No, I haven't heard it at all," you know, "heard about it at all."

And so the gay guy said, "Well, here, let me show you." And he said, "What you first have to do is you have to take a drink of your beer, and then you pull down your pants and touch the floor. And that's a touchdown. And if you want a field goal you have to fart. You fart for the field goal."

Well, the straight guy said, "*That's* the stupidest thing I've ever heard."

Well, the gay guy said, "No, it's a lot of fun. Let me show you." So he took his beer, he chugged it down, pulled down his pants and touched the floor: touchdown, six points. And then he let a good resounding one go—seven points because he got the field goal.

And so he was standing there, and the straight guy wasn't going to let *any gay* guy get one over on him. And so *he* took *his* beer, and he chugged it down, and pulled down his pants and touched the floor. So he had a touchdown, six points. But, you know, just as he was about to go for that field goal, the gay guy goes, "*Block* that *kick! Block* that *kick!*" [Teller thrusts hips back and forth, simulating intercourse.]

So that's the only one that I ever tell and the only one I can ever remember, because it gives the gays the good—the gays end up on the best side of that one.[10]

In this joke the straight man is conquered through cunning. The clever gay man tricks the other man into a position in which he can be pedicated, which many men would consider the ultimate humiliation.

There are also jokes in which straights are "put in their places" quite bluntly.

A very effeminate and faggoty homosexual was sitting in a truck stop bar, wearing tight pants, a fluffy sweater, and smoking a cigarette in a long, jeweled holder. A huge truckdriver [*sic*] comes in and sits next to the queen. The queen is instantly attracted to the rather surly man, so he decides to see if he can pick him up.

The homosexual tries to get the truckdriver's attention by blowing smoke in his face but this doesn't work. He then casually drops his cigarette holder and waits for the truckdriver to pick it up. Instead, the driver merely looks over at the homosexual and, after a pause, says, "Hey, fairy. You dropped your wand."

"*Well,*" thinks the homosexual, "this is going to be a toughy." But he is so attracted to the man that he tries again and drops the holder nearer the driver.

Again, the truckdriver just looks over and says, louder, "Hey, fairy! You dropped yer [*sic*] wand!"

"Oh, mercy," the homosexual laments. "He may get nasty but he's so *husky,* I've got to try to get this number. I'll try again."

This time, when the homosexual all but places the holder at the feet of the truckdriver, the driver gets to his feet and yells, "Hey, goddammit, you faggot! I said you dropped your wand!" The entire place is looking and snickering now.

Not being able to take any more, the queen, under the watchful eyes of all the drivers in the bar, curtsies down and picks up the jeweled holder, waves it at the irate truckdriver, and hisses, "Disappear, *bitch!*"[11]

This was about 1906 and this little fairy walks into uh this bar in San Francisco and he sits way at the end of the bar. And he, the bartender comes up to him and he says, "I'd like a martini." And the bartender comes up to him. He says, "We don't serve fairies or faggots in this place." So the little fairy is just infuriated and he just sits there with his legs crossed an' there at the bar and glares at the bartender. Just about that time the earthquake hits. My God, chandeliers falling, bottles falling behind the bar. Oh, it's complete chaos, people screaming. Then everything clears out. Everybody's running out an' the bartender's behind the bar all shook up you know, just shaking and he looks over across the bar and here the little fairy's still sittin' there glarin' at him. The little fairy says, "Now are you gonna serve me that martini or shall I do it again?" [All *sic*][12]

There was this little colored faggot that was cruising uh Selma Avenue and had been arrested five times for soliciting on Selma. So finally the fifth time why the Judge uh says, "Now look," he says, "It's five times now you've been arrested for the same thing." He says, "Uh, aren't you ashamed or something?" He says, "Wha, wha, wha, what's going on?" And the kid says, "Well Judge, you know how we is." The Judge says, "You know how we ARE." He says, "You too, Judge?"[13]

In the first two examples, presumed power is used to intimidate straights; in the third the straight authority figure is humiliated when the clever "colored faggot" deftly twists the judge's words to a new meaning. In all three instances it is the stereotypically effeminate homosexual man who triumphs over the stereotypically strong heterosexual man (the truck driver, the "macho" bartender, and the judge, strong in terms of authority if not physically powerful). It is significant that each joke stops at the point of the gay protagonist's victory, rather than going on to specify any response from the straight victim. Such a response would likely return power to the antagonist.

Gay power is also expressed in the following joke.

> Two gay men are sitting on the bank of the Ohio River down near Cincinnati, and this big ship comes by, loaded with cars and trucks. One of the guys says, "What's that?"
>
> And the other one says, "That's a ferry boat."
>
> The first one says, "Well, I *knew* we were organized, but I *damn sure* didn't know we had a navy!"[14]

Beneath the implied stupidity of one of the men lies another implication: "We will fight oppression and seek our freedom at all costs." Victory is achieved emotionally if not in fact, temporarily if not finally.

Jokes can also provide a sense of satisfaction in gay-straight relations by playing with the homophobia evident in heterosexual people's stereotypes of gays. The straight man's fear of homosexuality is the object of ridicule in this anecdote:

> I went to [a] church in Indianapolis last Sunday morning and I was surprised to find at the door a very macho man from Carmel who came to the door of the church at a very posh and elegant Episcopal church which is understated—Brooks Brothers—who, of course, was driving his usual northside Cadillac station wagon, and his family of seven kids and his lovely elegant wife standing behind him. He was wearing a purple crushed-velvet suit and a very fay appearance. I couldn't figure out why this was the case and I asked him, commenting on the amazing appearance of this strange-looking suit in [this] church, and he said, "Damn it, I told my wife to go to Cox's and get a seersucker suit."[15]

The man in the cocksucker suit is mortified, fearing he will be considered homosexual for wearing such an outrageous outfit. His situation is funny, but it is not the only humorous point in the story. The man is depicted as a fool because, despite his "predicament," he fails to learn from experience that not all men who appear effeminate are gay.

Farmer Jones is also afraid of homosexuality.

> This traveling salesman is looking for a place to stay because he's really tired and it's getting late. So he stops at this house and asks if they can give him a place to stay and something to eat. And the farmer says he's sorry, but he doesn't have any room. "But if you go on up the road about half a mile, I'm sure you can stay at Farmer Jones's, but I'd better warn you, he's sort of strange." The salesman said that didn't matter, he was so tired.
>
> So he went to Farmer Jones's and Farmer Jones said sure, he could

stay there. But they had just one rule: no one talked during supper. The first person to talk had to do the dishes. So they sat down and ate. Then they just sat there; and finally after forty-five minutes the salesman couldn't take it any longer. He jumped up, grabbed the farmer's beautiful daughter, and ravished her right there on the dining room floor. Nobody said anything. So they got up and sat down. About forty-five minutes later the salesman grabbed the farmer's wife, 'cause she wasn't too bad looking either, and pulled her down on the floor and ravished her. Nobody said anything. So they got up and as the salesman started to sit down he knocked over the candle and burned his arm. He ran up the stairs to the bathroom, screaming. He yelled down, "Where's the Vaseline?" The farmer said, "Never mind, I give up. I'll do the dishes."

In this prose version of "Get Up and Bar the Door" (Child 275),[16] Farmer Jones is shown to be the ultimate chauvinist. He is willing to sacrifice his wife's and daughter's "honor" to avoid undertaking a "woman's job" (doing dishes). He ultimately relinquishes part of his masculine image, however, to save his masculinity; it is better to be less than totally masculine than to be emasculated. His fear stems only partly from a presumption of impending homosexual rape; it is based on his stereotype of gays as predatory creatures preoccupied with sex. He is also seen as a fool because he jumps to conclusions based on little evidence. Had he given the matter any thought, Farmer Jones would have realized that in yelling for Vaseline the salesman had been the first to speak and was thus obligated to do the dishes.

Again we see that humor can easily serve to hold stereotypes of homosexuality up to ridicule; by invalidating common misconceptions, jokes validate gay culture and allow gay people to feel better about themselves.

One aspect of gay humor that is particularly difficult to define is *camp,* one of those words whose meaning is known but elusive when one attempts to verbalize it. The problem of definition is compounded by the many authors who base their explanations of camp on effeminacy.[17]

In her well-known article "Notes on 'Camp,'" Susan Sontag says, "Camp sees everything in quotation marks." Alan Brien, in "Camper's Guide," makes a similar statement: "Camp . . . [is] the habit of speaking almost entirely in italics, of tarting up ideas with costume jewellery." According to Michael Monroe, "Camp is when you apply an inappropriate degree of sophistication to a subject." And Leonard R. N. Ashley says, "*Camp* is clever as well as rude, tacky and bitchy, cute and cynical, merry and merciless, at its best when it has enough salt in it to preserve it."[18] Statements about camp go on ad infinitum but do not give a thorough, succinct explanation of the concept. Most authors have overlooked its serious nature, Sontag even argues that camp displays an "insistence on not being 'serious.'"[19] Therefore, I offer this definition:

Camp is an attitude, a style of humor, an approach to situations, people, and things. The camp point of view is assertively expressed through exaggeration and inversion, stressing form over content,[20] deflating pomposity, mocking pretension, and subverting values. Camp is the manifestation of a "tension between [a] person or thing and [its] context or association."[21] Sometimes (but certainly not always) camp behavior is effeminate. Like much gay humor, camp plays with stereotypes, carrying them to extremes, flouting heterosexual values. Camp shows the world "as it could be,"[22] while saying, "My God, what if it *were* that way?" Camp is a metacultural statement, an aspect of culture commenting on culture. Camp can be solely playful, but often it is a serious medium, providing a weapon against oppression.

Edmund White explains the aggressiveness of camp:

By declaring that bad art is good, tackiness tasteful, the camp vogue announces its dictatorial power—the power to switch all minuses to pluses and vice-versa. Not *all,* for the hierarchy of camp excellence is arbitrary and unsystematic. . . . Because camp is so arbitrary, it frightens the uninitiated or at least makes them uneasy. I would claim that the *function* of camp is to promote such uneasiness; it is a muted, irresponsible form of antagonism, one too silly to be held accountable, *a safe way of subverting the system.*[23]

Camp was and is basically a gay phenomenon. The term *camp,* in the sense that it is used here, has been in use at least since the 1890s. (Brien suggests that the word "derives from the French verb *se camper,* which means 'to posture boldly' and was used of actors in heroic melodrama.'")[24] In the 1960s, the period of radical chic, "Notes on Camp" almost surely played a role in bringing the style to the attention of the liberal parts of the heterosexual culture. Camp is not limited to the gay subculture, and it is not "synonymous with homosexual taste," as Esther Newton claims in *Mother Camp.* On the other hand, Sontag presumes too much when she says, "Camp taste is much more than homosexual taste. . . . Yet one feels that if homosexuals hadn't more or less invented Camp, someone else would." If such were the case, straights would have discovered camp long before the 1960s. The author of "Vest-Pocket Guide to Camp" is closer to the mark:

Homosexuals, who always have had a vested interest in knocking down bourgeois standards, are in the vanguard of Camp, though no longer its sole custodians. In fact, the word Camp was '20s slang for homosexual both here and in England and was evolved by homosexuals to its current meaning of exaggerated style.[25]

Some examples of camp will help to clarify the meaning of the word. If a scholarly work on homosexuality were to be published on lavender paper, its seriousness would be called into question by the colored paper—despite there being no correlation between color and content—and the result would be campy. In doing background reading for this study at the Alfred C. Kinsey Institute for Research in Sex, Gender, and Reproduction, I was looking through the vertical file folder labeled "Homosexual Drag." The first item was a mimeographed flyer announcing the Miss Gay Philadelphia Drag Ball; the rest of the contents of the folder were programs for the Vienna Boys' Choir. That was camp, the implication being that the choirboys were in drag. The campiness was compounded by my discovery taking place in an internationally known center for the serious study of sexuality. Finally, in the spring of 1987, someone stomped several goslings to death in an Indianapolis neighborhood that has a large number of resident ducks and geese. Shortly thereafter, someone planted a small cross beside the canal where the goslings had been killed. Reminiscent of the crosses placed at the sites of fatal automobile accidents, the memorial in this case implied—contrary to most Christian theologies—that animals have souls and that the deaths of the goslings were the equivalent of human deaths.

Vito Russo gives another example of camp. His article "Camp" is not only about camp; much of the tone of the article is campy, as the following passage illustrates.

> The best camp will remain affectionate and naive. . . . The next time Queen Elizabeth has a luncheon, watch it on television. She arrives from her upstairs bedroom and enters her own dining room with a smart little leather handbag hanging from her arm. That Queen is such a camp.[26]

Note Russo's pun in the last sentence: *Queen* refers to Elizabeth II, but the phrase "that queen is such a camp" is a typical gay line used to refer to a person for whom the description is appropriate. And is there a campy implication here that the queen is actually a drag queen?

Interestingly, a number of famous women are camp figures for the gay subculture, cult heroines as it were. Women like Tallulah Bankhead, Mae West, Judy Garland, and Joan Crawford, along with others like them, are revered and imitated. These women were glamorous, strong, distinctive, and quick witted. As Marc Henderson suggests, "They were glamorous men in some ways." Regarding Tallulah Bankhead, John Herrick says, "In her public behavior she was what we all were at our cocktail parties behind closed doors." In other words, these women had a freedom not allowed gays. Michael Monroe sums it up, saying,

> **They had style. . . . We know them by their public persona, which was a result of their training as actresses to exude a certain—that persona, which they stylized and—or which *we* stylized; it became a style through our perception of it—and it worked. It was finely tuned, it was rehearsed, it was flawless, and therefore, very beguiling. Everybody wants to be able to live their life as though it were a movie. You wouldn't have the missed cues and stumbled blocking.[27]**

A cycle of stories has developed around Tallulah Bankhead, drawing on her reputation for flouting social standards. In the following example, Bankhead is used to express the disdain many gays have for organized religion, one of the major oppressors of homosexual people.

Tallulah Bankhead was, as everybody knows, a very faithful communi-
cant of the Episcopal church, and went to Saint Mary the Virgin in New
York, which is the highest church in the Anglican communion in this
country. And she was seated next to the aisle, and as the procession
came in, the thurifer led the way—the thurifer is the person who swings
the thurible or incense pot—and she reached out and grabbed him as he
came by, saying, "I love the drag, honey, but your purse is on fire."[28]

As in the story about Browning and Kipling discussed in chapter 2, Bankhead is
saying here, "I know the score." The thurifer, adorned in gaudy robes and
swinging the thurible on jingling chains, is to her the epitome of a drag queen.

Bankhead's cleverness of response is evident in other anecdotes as well. For
example,

"With your deep voice, Miss Bankhead, has anyone ever mistaken you
for a man?"
"No, darling. Has anyone ever made the mistake with you?"[29]

This anecdote, emphasizing the masculine aspects of Bankhead's personality, is
also a mild put-down of effeminate gays. The potential offense is mitigated by
Bankhead's strong personality and its implication that she was a female impersonator (a notion also attached to Mae West). This implication is made strongly
in another example.

When asked if a certain young man were gay, Tallulah Bankhead responded, "Why how should I know, dahling? He never has sucked *my*
dick."[30]

While underscoring Bankhead's masculine characteristics, this quip makes the
statement that sexuality is a private matter, and that the questioner has no right
to ask for such information.

The apparent homophobia in another Bankhead story can be understood in a
similar way.

Tallulah and [another actress] went for a ride in the country. And [the
other woman] said, "Tallulah, you're just going to *have* to stop the car. I
have to pee." So Tallulah stopped the car and [her friend] went off in the
bushes to pee. And while she was peeing this snake slithered up and bit
her on the twat. And she thought, "Oh, my God! *What* am I going to do?"
So she called Tallulah and said, "*Tallulah,* you're going to *have* to go into
town and find a doctor. A *snake* has bitten me on the twat!"
So Tallulah got back into the car and drove back to town and found a
doctor and said, "Doctor, the most *dreadful* thing has happened. A *snake*
has bitten my *dear* friend . . . on the *twat. What* are we *going* to do?"
And the doctor said, "Well, you're going to have to go back out to the
woods and take a big bite out of it and suck out all the poison."
So Tallulah got back in the car and drove back out to the woods and

got out of the car and [her friend] said, *"Tallulah, what* did the *doctor* say?"

And Tallulah said, "He said you're going to die, dahling."

Bankhead's aversion to engage in what could be construed as a lesbian act to save her friend's life might be seen as a homophobic reaction. On the other hand, the story could be popular among gay men because of the imagined possibility that Bankhead was a gay man in drag, in which case (s)he would be disgusted by the thought of cunnilingus or anything resembling that act.

Bankhead's sexual orientation itself is the subject of the following story.

Tallulah and [her friend] were putting some new black and white curtains up in Tallulah's apartment. Tallulah was on the ladder and [her friend] was holding it steady. All of a sudden Tallulah slipped and fell on top of [her friend], with the curtains in a heap on top of them. Tallulah started laughing hysterically. [Her friend] said, "Tallulah! What are you laughing about?" And Tallulah said, "Oh, I'm just remembering those two nuns we had in the back seat of the car."

In this example, Bankhead and her friend are reputed to be lesbians, thus offering another explanation of their popularity in the gay subculture: they are considered a legitimate part of the community.

A third story involving Bankhead and her friend is a comment on violating cultural norms.

Tallulah and [another actress] were in the elevator and [the friend] looked over at Tallulah and said, "Tallulah! Did you fart?" And Tallulah said, "Why of course, dahling. Do you think I always smell like this?"

Bankhead has broken two taboos, one by passing gas in another person's presence and another by admitting her flatulence. Her friend, in turn, has violated a third taboo by forcing Bankhead to acknowledge her lapse. Having been caught in a potentially embarrassing situation in which the identity of the farter is obvious to both parties, Tallulah turns flatus into status with her clever response. In this way Bankhead is able to enjoy a freedom from the norms that most people (including gays) are expected to uphold.

It is much easier for the famous and the infamous to flout conventions than it is for most people. Gay people in a sense occupy a privileged social status in that they are *expected* to be outrageous. Thus Bankhead can serve as a role model and can be admired. Sharing such a model and stories about her justifies the theme of rebellion present in much gay folklore and behavior. Justification, in turn, reinforces the group sense of worth, for if behavior is validated it must be both good and acceptable.

Personal experience stories form another group of narratives among gay men. Identity is generally established before sharing such experiences. Since the narratives involved are usually extremely personal, telling them makes the narrator vulnerable, and sharing them indicates a sense of intimacy, a bond. They also, as James P. Leary points out, "impress upon the minds of participants gathered in private social roles the behavioral strategies to be applied or avoided in subsequent public situations."[31] These stories offer advice, support, and counseling, serving as a sort of folk psychiatry. Sandra K. D. Stahl writes,

> The conventions of the story make self-revelation acceptable and entertaining, but the courage of the storyteller in articulating usually covert values makes the storytelling an engaging experience, for the teller and the audience. In effect the narrator tests personal values—practical, moral, social, aesthetic—with every story repetition.[32]

Coming-out stories make up one of the major subdivisions of gay personal experience narratives. Coming out is an experience all openly gay people share, and since it is a continuing process, many people have more than one narrative about coming out. This experience is potentially quite traumatic, and thus is imbued with fear and apprehension. The stories give people considering coming out examples of how to do so, how not to do so, and what to expect upon doing so. To have come out is an accomplishment; it is to have met a challenge; it is probably the most significant rite of passage of the gay experience. The narratives are sometimes funny, sometimes sad, sometimes uplifting, often poignant, and frequently retold. Edmund White, referring to a group telling personal experience narratives, points out that "they were all familiar with each other's sagas, but they were eager to hear every word again."[33]

The next two narratives, related by Steve Daniels, are typical coming-out stories. In the first one Steve uses a long introduction, as do many narrators, to set the story within its proper biographical framework. Steve also explains why he tells other people about this experience. The second story is about a friend's acknowledgment of Steve's homosexuality.

Steve: It must have been my first or second year of college—I don't remember. I had met a man. He was older and he owned a flower shop here in town. We'd become lovers, and during one of the summer breaks from school I'd moved in with him. Then when it came time [that] I was supposed to move back home, my mom just sort of like [said], "Well, you're not moving home are you?" And I said, "Well, probably not."

Then [we] had lived together—I don't remember—a couple of years, probably. . . . And [my older brother] had sold insurance to these friends of ours. Well, this friend was a real effeminate person—[he] was just a *screamer*. I mean, there's no other word for it. . . . [His] lover was like in his late forties and [he] was about my age. And he'd gotten life insurance, but his lover was paying for it and everything. Well even my brother was smart enough to realize they were gay. And so he'd gone around and he'd told my—he'd gone to my father and he'd told my father that he thought I was queer, and that it was my mom's fault. Then he went to both of my older sisters and told them the same thing.

I'd lived with [my lover] long enough and I'd gotten to the place where I was uncomfortable—because I never lied to them. I never pretended that

I went on dates or anything else, because I didn't like pretending that way, and I wouldn't do that, but I felt uncomfortable not even being able to really talk. I was pretty sure my mom would accept it, but I didn't know about my dad, 'cause he, like, has been a factory worker all his life and kind of—just, we'd never really gotten along real well, so I wasn't too hot on the idea of telling him.

But I'd kind of gotten to the place where I was going to tell my parents, and my brother . . . went around, told the whole family. Well, the way he did it was enough to basically turn everybody against him, and it wouldn't have mattered much what he was saying about me, because he pissed my mom off because he told her it was her fault, and he—basically my sisters both told him it was none of his business, and one of them asked him to leave her house and not come back till he was invited.

So anyhow, my parents had mentioned this, what he'd said and—one night [my lover] and I had taken my mother and father and my younger brother out for dinner for my mom's birthday. We'd gone to the country club and we'd all had a lot to drink. It was real bizarre. We left the country club and we were all feeling no pain, and my dad wanted to take us all to the V.F.W., because—I'd never been to the V.F.W., I hadn't had any real *desire* to go to the V.F.W., but he just wanted to take us. And of course [my lover] was a—he would make it sound like he wanted to go whether he did or not. So Dad was going to take us to the V.F.W.

We got there and my little brother started sucking down all these drinks because the waitress was—I don't know what her problem was—but anyhow she kept bringing all these drinks that no one had ordered, and he kept drinking them all. Well, he got sick, so I took him and [my lover] over to our apartment, and then I went back to get Mom and Dad. And, they started talking, and they said something about, "What your brother said about you." And I said, "You mean about being homosexual?" And they said yes, and I said, "Well, I am what I am, and I'm not going to change."

And they both said, "Well, we realize that, and we love you." They had some concerns about whether or not I would ever be happy. And my mother was like, "Well, I know it's going to be a harder life than if you were straight."

We talked about it some that night, and I don't remember a lot of it, 'cause I was getting real loaded. But anyhow, we've talked quite a bit since then. At first it was a little strained. I could talk better with my mom than I could with my dad, but it's gotten to the place now where—at one point, because of financial reasons [my lover] and I lived with my parents. I couldn't ask for a more loving, supporting family than I've gotten. It's really great.

Joe: Do you tell other people about this experience?

Steve: Yes—because there are a lot of gay people that are so afraid that—their families finding out that they're gay, 'cause a lot of times you hear the horror stories of so-and-so's parents found out, and disowned him, and threw him out, and all these things. So, it's kind of like, by relating my experiences, hopefully [I'll] kind of make them a little less fearful

[of] talking with their families, 'cause it's been, probably one of the best things that ever happened to me.

Steve: There's an older lady that through the store I got to be really good friends with. She'd bought some things there and she was redoing a house. It was a big old farmhouse that she—her husband had some money and they like tripled its size. And we got to be really good friends. And for a long time I really didn't talk to her about being gay. It was obvious that she knew just by the way that she talked about [my lover] and I.

One of the times—I'd go over there and chat for hours. And I was over there and I was getting ready to leave, and I said I had to go. She asked me what I was fixing for supper. And I said, "I'm not fixing *anything* for supper," because [my lover] had been to cooking school in Germany and he did all the cooking, and I never *did* cook with him.

And she was like, "You mean you don't have to go home and fix dinner?" And I said no. And she said, "Well, if I didn't fix dinner for *my* husband he'd throw me out in the street." [Laughs.]

I [said] like, "*Well* he's *not* my husband, and *he* does the cooking."[34]

Steve's coming out to his parents was something he had wanted to do for some time, but it was actually precipitated by his brother's actions. One of the messages implicit in Steve's story is this: because gays have learned to keep their homosexuality secret to avoid all sorts of abuse—both psychological and physical—it is difficult for them to reveal their orientation even to those closest to them, family and friends whom they would freely trust in other matters. Steve's parents express the same concerns most parents express for their children, gay or straight: they want them to be happy. Their response makes it clear that gays frequently give straights little credit for being open and understanding.

Steve's second narrative is an example of coming out without really coming out. Through her statement, "Well, if I didn't fix dinner for *my* husband he'd throw me out in the street," Steve's friend is saying, "I know you're gay, and so you don't have to tell me. It's all right. It doesn't bother me, and I don't want you to feel uncomfortable about it." Her acceptance, like that of Steve's parents, is somewhat surprising since she is straight. Her understanding of gay life, however, is based to an extent on stereotypes. She implies that Steve's lover is his "husband" and that Steve is the "wife" in the relationship. Many straights share this misconception, assuming that gay relationships parallel straight marriages—one partner taking the male role, the other taking the female role, both in domestic affairs and in bed.

Steve's comment about telling others of his coming out to help them feel better about the process explains the cohesive nature of such narratives. Working to help each other overcome problems and deal with awkward situations—coming together in times of difficulty and stress—are hallmarks of cohesion.

Sometimes coming-out stories deal with self-discovery, as in the following one, told by John Herrick.

John: I grew up in a part of the world where you knew a lot about animals and therefore you knew a lot about *sex* very early in your life. You heard all this stuff. I was always around boys somewhat older than myself, and I'd hear all these things. And I heard things like "seduction," and I somehow got the sense that seduction had to do with leading people into doing things they shouldn't do, wouldn't do if you didn't trick them. And of course I was the head altar boy, and I just couldn't understand how you could do that.

I went to a movie, and I don't remember—I was eleven years old—I don't remember what the movie was. I don't remember an awful lot about it. I do remember Carmen Miranda in one of her *most* elaborate headgears, and the incomparable Lena Horne. And she did—I'll *see* her till the day I die—I will *hear* her. She wore a very simple white chiffon dress. You know, it was one of these that had no bodice, just a couple of straps. And it came to—it was close-fitting to the waist, and it had a full skirt, just below the knees. And she had on red strap shoes, and there was a narrow red patent-leather belt, and here at one side, a bunch of artificial violets. *Stunning* costume. (Of course she still is an incredibly beautiful creature.) She leaned against this pillar. She made very few movements. And she sang "Stormy Weather." I remember how I fancied her voice. And I sat in the theater, and I watched her, and I listened to her, and I identified fully with her. And then I had this *wonderful* illumination, and I understood seduction, and I knew how it worked.

Not long after—have I ever told you about our gardener?

Joe: No.

John: We had a playhouse. It had two rooms. It was quite a sizable structure; an adult could stand up in it. And in the back room there was this big, old, Saratoga-type trunk that my mother had put there so my sister could put her dress-up clothes in it. You know, my sister would get all these *things* that my mother didn't wear anymore and she'd put them in there, and she and her friends would go in and they'd have their dress-up things. And sometimes when they were staging a wedding or something and they needed an extra bridesmaid they'd drag me in and dress me up.

Well, anyway, along about the time of that Lena Horne movie, my parents hired this handyman and gardener. His name was Shorty; I mean that's [the only name] I knew for him. He was beautiful. He was twenty-one, or twenty-two, twenty-three. He was a really hot case as we say now—a term we didn't have in those days. And I was smitten!

And I saw the Lena Horne movie, and I kept thinking about Shorty. And now that I knew what seduction was all about, I had to figure out how to do it. But, you know, it was hard to translate the *understanding* I had from the movie to *my* life, because Lena Horne was a woman. And *then* it hit me: you become a woman!

So, at this point in the development of my sister and my brother and

I—and my sister was older. My brother was always very masculine and outgoing. I don't think he was *ever* in that playhouse more than three or four times in his whole life. And my sister had stopped using it, so it was essentially my private domain.

This one day, Shorty was working in the rose garden, which was very near the front door of the playhouse—which door could not be seen from the house, by the way. So I went into the playhouse, and—I went back, and I had—I remember I had the *specific* garment in mind, because I had always loved my mother in it, and regretted when she gave it up. It was a dinner gown, and it consisted of a black silk sheath, over which there was this chiffon—very simple, not, you know, yards and yards and yards, and really cut very slinky—outer dress kind of thing. So—it was pulled in at the waist. It was quite an elegant gown.

I went into the playhouse and found the closest thing to high heels I could find there. It wasn't very good, because my mother was very tall and in high heels would be taller than my father, so she didn't wear them. But I did the best I could. And I removed every stitch of clothing I had on. And I put on these shoes, and I omitted the black silk sheath. I just put on this net. [Laughs.] And I rolled up Lipton's tea in some notebook paper! And I stood in the doorway, sultry, smoking my Lipton tea cigarette. [Laughter.] And Shorty looked at me and he said, "Johnny, what are you doing?"

I can hear myself saying, "I thought I'd invite you in for tea. Would you like some?" And he said yes. And he came in, and of course the only tea to be served was *me*. [Laughter.] And he liked it, and he came every day for a year and a half until we got caught. [Laughter.][35]

John has developed a coherent narrative containing several apparent digressions that in actuality are details essential to the plot. In the story he comes to an awareness of himself, and ultimately is brought out (as opposed to coming out) when he is discovered. The humor and wistfulness of the narrative combine to give a poignant and revealing picture of life as a gay adolescent. John's sharing of this story creates a bond of intimacy between him and his audience, since he usually reveals such details of his past only to those he feels close to.

Discovery can take many forms. Hal Parmenter describes a very traumatic instance.

Following college I went to seminary—I guess at the age of twenty-one—where I *instantly* fell in love with a guy and had a wonderful time. It was highly mutual and my first great love affair. . . . I was in the throes of a grand and glorious love affair which I still do not regret. And my first lover, named Jack, was a beautiful guy who happened to be from another Indiana State Teachers College—the one in Pennsylvania. We had everything in common, and we were both bright in a class that was made up exclusively of people from Harvard, Yale, Dartmouth, and Princeton, one Colgate man and one William and Mary person. The result was that Jack and I studied together, and one thing led to another.

We finally couldn't resist making love, which was done at 3:20 in the afternoon on the seventeenth day of February in the year 1959. It was a glorious and happy occasion.

My next-door neighbor . . . had a tape recorder and made a tape recording of Jack and me in bed. He took it to one of the officials of the school, who called me into his office.

Now, remember, in those days it was awkward to have violated any kind of social customs or any kind of sexual laws. And frankly I think that everybody was aware that Jack and I were having a fling, and it was the most pronounced, or socially obvious fling going on in seminary. It certainly wasn't the only one.

So, I went to see the official of the school, who had the tape recorder sitting on his desk, and there were several faculty people sitting around. And I kept wondering why those particular faculty people, because Jack and I had discussed the proclivities of many of the people in the community. The official played the tape, I was embarrassed, and *he* was embarrassed, I think everybody in the room was embarrassed.

Because he'd been very well brought up he turned the tape off, and he said, "I think you understand what that is." And I said, "Yes." He said, "I just want to welcome you to the Club," and he reached across the desk and shook my hand.

I, needless to say, had been thinking about how I was going to resign with saving face, and how I was going to be let out of the school with honor. And in fact I discovered that I had entered into a holy of holies.

So the result was that as time went by I discovered that the Club is a very powerful and controlling influence in the life of the church. I do not think this is cynical; I think it is absolutely a political truth. I have seen since then many bishops and clergy elected to important cures because of their membership in the Club.

But the *implication* was—and this I mark as my great public coming out, because I came out to my public, my club, and in a sense it was done for me; I really believe that the Club has existed—but the implication in his shaking hands and in his saying, "Welcome to the Club," the message was, "Be discreet, be closety. You can find *us*"—that is, your support group, or your system, or your people to care about—"any place you want to look." And I found that to be true. All of which is pretty neat.[36]

After being brought out, Hal fortunately found that he was not alone and was not an outcast. Rather he learned that he was one among many and that being out was not a great disaster. Indeed, this point is one of the basic messages of coming-out stories. What statement can be more supportive and more cohesive than, "You are not alone"? Those who share narratives of this sort are living proof that despite the difficulties life can be enjoyed, even (and perhaps more) when one's homosexuality is no longer a secret.

Ramona Halston, a female impersonator, tells of another case of being discovered.

I was buying lipstick and a blush one time and a little boy came up to me. I guess he was like nine or ten, I'm not sure, but he was that small. He walked up to me, and—I had on clogs and he said, "Are you a girl or a boy?"

And I said, "I'm a boy."

And he said, "Why do you have on girls' shoes?"

And I said, "Well, these are boys' shoes."

And he said, "No, my sister has those. Those are *girls'* shoes."

"No, these are *boys'* shoes."

Then he said, "Well, if you're a boy, why are you buying makeup?"

And I said, "Well, I want to buy it."

He said, "Do you wear it?"

And I said, "Mm hm." [Laughter.]

And he said, "Are you one of those punk rockers?"

And I said, "Uh, yes, that's what I am. I'm a punk rocker."

And he said, "Oh, like the B-52's."

And I said, "Yes, like the B-52's." And I'm thinking, *"Please,* little boy," you know, "go on down the aisle with your mother." So he was satisfied with that. He was satisfied that I was a punk rocker and that's why I was buying makeup.

And then I had to buy hose. So when I got to the check-out counter I had this makeup and hose laid out there, and this little boy runs up and says, *"Hose?* Punk rockers don't wear hose." And then he looks up at the guy who's checking me out and says, "This guy's a faggot. I've been giv-ing him trouble back here. Tried to tell me he was a punk rocker and I know he's not." [Laughter.]

And then I just kind of looked at this little kid like, "I *can't* believe you." And this kid was so—he only looked nine or ten, and he just—"This guy's a faggot and he's trying to tell me he's a punk rocker." [Laughs.][37]

In this instance Ramona thought she had managed to avoid discovery, only to find out later that her secret was known after all. (I use feminine pronouns here following female impersonators' standard usage.) The point, however, beyond the humor of the story, is that Ramona's exposure was not a particularly bad experience; rather it now serves as an entertaining story to share with friends who can understand her panic and embarrassment and who can have some of their own fears alleviated by sharing vicariously in Ramona's predicament.

There are also personal experience narratives about love affairs. Hal Parmen-ter gives the following example.

This is precious to me, and I wouldn't want to make light of it.

When I was in school, when I was in seminary, one of our professors was Paul Tillich's secretary, who spoke only German, and a little bit of French. We sat at a table that spoke French, back in those days when I could do it. And at one session he asked in French, what did I have as my greatest dream in life. And I said, "If I had my druthers, I would love to spend a day of my life from early morning until late at night lying on the side of a fell in the Lake District in England and read Romantic poetry all day long, and drink wine, eat cheese, and weep. And afterwards, he kind of sullied my image by saying, "Ah, that would be very good, Mr. Parmenter, if only you had just had sex."

And so, many years later, my lover . . . and I went to England, and we started out from the Old England Hotel in Boness and went to an off-license shop and bought a bottle of wine, a loaf of bread, and some cheese; went to the Dove Cottage of Wordsworth and bought volumes of Romantic English poetry; and we lay on the side of a fell and looked at the Lake Country, spread out small below us, and we had sex, and we cried, and we read poetry to each other, and we picked clover, and we ate bread and cheese and drank wine all day, and cried a lot. And it still is very beautiful to me.

That's a true story. It was the culmination of my dream; my romantic dream was apeak at that point, and I don't have another romantic dream of that nature to replace it with. It's terrible at the age of thirty-eight or whatever I was to have achieved your life's goal. It was quite beautiful.

Here is another of Hal's stories:

Once upon a time [my ex-lover] and I were in Myrtle Beach, South Carolina—our first great bawdy trip, which was one-hundred-percent sex all over the United States. . . . And I had written ahead, got a very lovely room overlooking the beach. It was right *on* the beach. Very expensive room in a motel. When we got there we were shown an ugly room near the front of the motel, near the street. And I said, "Don't you have a room in the back? I asked specifically for the room by the beach."

And he said, "Oh, you wouldn't want that room; it's very big and it's got a kitchen and it costs more."

I said, "It sounds exactly [like] what we want."

And he said, "Well, it's also the place where the air conditioning equipment is for the entire motel."

I said, "That's OK; we don't mind listening to air conditioners, it's hot."

And they said, "OK, but you might get interrupted."

Well, we were.

And we'd gone to—we didn't have much cash with us, as I remember; that was a long time ago—and so we decided to buy one king-size sheet for the bed instead of two regular size sheets, because it would be cheaper. So we bought a big king-size sheet and we wrote each other love notes on it in very heavy indelible ink, which I still have.

Every time we started any kind of sexual activity, the door would simply open and in would walk a workman to take care of something with the air conditioner. And [my lover] was particularly shy in those days, and I was not *terribly* pleased about the interruption. But it was an invariable thing. It makes it sound as if we were having sex ninety percent of the time, and maybe we were in fact. But it was a fun and kind of pleasant memory at this point. But it wasn't very funny at the time. We were angry about being interrupted. [My lover] was *very* upset.

[He] also would invariably go around when we were in various hotels and mess up the other bed to make it look as if he'd slept in a different bed. [Laughter.] I kept wondering why, because we weren't exactly unobvious.[38]

As Hal points out himself, the first narrative reveals his romanticism; the second one does too, for that matter—requesting a room by the beach and writing love notes to each other on the sheet. The tenderness evident in the first example is heightened by the bucolic setting, expressed succinctly in the line "we lay on the side of a fell and looked at the Lake Country, spread out small below us." This tone contributes a great deal to conveying that the story is indeed precious to the narrator. In addition, it shows that romantic love is possible between two men, contradicting a common misconception held by many people, including a lot of gay men. By contributing to the overall mental health of the gay community and to its members' individual self-images, messages such as this one further strengthen the bonds of gay unity.

Sexual exploits and misadventures are topics of personal experience narratives as well. Ramona Halston relates a cautionary tale.

Ramona: It was the summer right after I came out. And I guess I had only had, I had only been to bed with two different guys before that. And both of them were—well, the first one I only saw that one night, and I just—I thought everything that he tried was gross. [Laughs.] The second one was the guy that I was seeing for a while.

But then that summer I was supposed to meet two friends on the block [a local cruising area]. And I was waiting for them and a guy came up to the car window and asked me, you know, "What are you doing?" The usual stuff, you know. "What's happening? What are you doing? Where are you going? Who are you waiting on?" Just all this little talk. And I wasn't—I mean I wasn't interested. I'm just trying to put him off so he'll leave.

And he reached inside the car and took the car keys. And then he and another guy, a guy who was with him, got me *out* of my car and into theirs, and took me to [a local motel]. And I was like, "Oh, my God! What is going to happen now?" [Laughs.]

I ended up in the room with one guy, and my first instinct was to scream [laughter], because he was much bigger than I was. Like, I don't know, he was much taller, bigger, muscular, and—as much fighting as I was doing it wasn't helping at all. And so I thought, "Well, I'll scream." And then it came to mind that, "I work in a public library, in a children's department, and if I scream, people are going to come running into this room, and they're going to find *me* with *him,* and its going to look just as bad on me as it will on"—you know, I mean, it's going to look bad for my job in other words—the publicity or whatever might happen.

So, I kept thinking, "I *have* to get him back somehow while he's doing all this stuff." And at the time I had—this, it's gross. [Laughter.] I think it's funny, but it's gross. I had been really sick just a few days before with the flu, and so I had diarrhea. [Laughter.] I thought, "I *have* to get him back." And so I just *shit everyplace*. [Laughter.] It was all over me, and him, and the bed, and everything. It wasn't as bad for me as it was for him. He didn't like it too well. [Laughs.] Hit me a few times. But then, after everything was over, at least I felt like I got him back somehow! [Laughter.] 'Cause he *didn't* enjoy that. So he did let me take a shower and drove me back to my car and gave me my car keys. . . .

Joe: Why do you tell that story?

Ramona: Mostly now—at first it was—I think the first few times that I told it there had been a few people beaten up on the block. And someone had just made the comment that, "Oh, that never happens. I've never seen anything like that happen."

And I just said, you know, "Look, *it happens!* Let me tell you, it happens." And just told them what happened. Everybody's reaction is the same way—they think it's *hilarious* that I reacted that way to him.[39]

Some of the dangers gay people face are vividly expressed in Ramona's story. Gays frequently must resort to surreptitious means of meeting people; they cannot always be sure they are safe around people they have just met. Ramona underscores this fact with her story. The narrative also has a satisfying ending, since one of the abductors is humiliated when Ramona gets even with him. Once again Ramona tells her listeners that all gay people share fears, but that problems—even gay ones—can be overcome.

Hal Parmenter relates an experience of his that had a less-than-satisfactory outcome.

I have a great propensity to fall in love. I have a tremendous propensity to fall in love with organists. And I had—as [pastor of a church in another city] I had the world's most beautiful organist, without any question. . . . He was twenty-seven at that time, and I had always wanted to have a thing with [him. We] would have never managed as long as he was working for me. I think probably both of us were aware of our responsibility to the church and to God in that regard.

But when I moved to another city he shortly . . . became the assistant organist at [a church] in New York. When [my ex-lover] and I went to New York, I decided—because [my organist] and I the previous winter had had a little *diner à deux* at Lutèce in New York, which was very nice but it cost six hundred and some dollars. And I kind of had a hope at that moment that we would have a little fling, but it didn't work out. We both got too drunk.

We [had gone] to Lutèce, and it was *very* elegant. *I mean elegant;* I'd had reservations for two months. It's a very hard restaurant to get a reservation for. It is a restaurant in which one speaks French exclusively; they do not speak English there at all, and there is no menu. It is all ordered directly from the waiter, who speaks *elegant* French rapidly, and I didn't understand it.

But we nevertheless did order. And things would catch as they zoomed by in French. And I heard "pâté of lark," so we ordered pâté of lark. And if you can imagine pâté of lark livers—it required undoubtedly thirty-five or fifty larks to make enough pâté. I regret this at this point because they are even an endangered species, but the fact is that I personally killed off thirty-five larks for this pâté. The lark liver cost $125 for two, and it was worth it. I would never order it again, but it was certainly the most elegant spendthrift thing I've ever done. The dinner cost $625 for two, and it was worth every penny of it.

Suffice it, the following summer [my ex-lover] and I went to New York, stayed in the Plaza in a suite for a lot of money a night. And it was gorgeous, and it was *totally* respectable. [My lover] wasn't, but *it* was. And so he and I took [the organist] out to dinner. And then after dinner we were relaxed and not drunk. We came back to the hotel—for a night-cap, supposedly. And things all just seemed to work out without anybody's saying anything, that allowed us to go to bed together—all of us. It was the first and only time that [my lover] and I ever did a three-way, and the only time that I was ever in bed with [the organist].

But the *problem* was, as I very rapturously undressed the young man, [I] discovered that he had a bent cock. And he was very aroused. And the more he got aroused, the "benter" his cock got. And it ultimately stabbed him in the abdomen. And he—I—to this day I still can't figure out what to do with it. It's terribly sad. And it was the culmination as it were of a five-year wish. And it was a disaster. It was a very sad moment. We didn't know what to do. We did an awful lot of touching and playing around, but ultimately [my lover] and I wound up together as usual. And we all sort of looked at [the organist] and said, "Sorry."[40]

In this narrative, in addition to fostering cohesiveness by sharing such intimate details of his life and making himself vulnerable by leaving himself open to ridicule or reproach from his audience, Hal confronts two fears common among gay men. First is the anxiety over the possibility of sexual failure, a concern of many straight men as well. Although the failure in this case is not the result of impotence, the failure is none the less real. The second and related (though less obvious) fear addressed is the possibility of rejection. This fear is heightened among gays because of the rejection they experience in society and often from their friends and families. Hal does not express these fears openly, but they lie just below the surface. After five years he finally almost achieved what he wanted, only to meet with failure. And yet he is willing to share this experience with others to show them that it is normal to be afraid, and it is all right to fail: neither makes one less of a man than he was before.

Female impersonation is another subject around which is grouped a number of traditions. Drag is not paralleled in other subcultures and it is highly visible; as a result, female impersonators often find themselves in situations likely to result in experiences suitable for narrative formation.

Esther Newton may be right when she says, "Drag and camp are the most representative and widely used symbols of homosexuality in the English speaking world,"[41] but if so it is only because these manifestations of gay culture are more noticeable than the more common aspects of gay life.

Newton also claims that drag maintains "that the sex-role system really is natural: therefore homosexuals are unnatural." This statement is incorrect. Newton in fact contradicts herself, writing elsewhere, "The gay world, via drag, says that sex-role behavior is an appearance; it is 'outside.' It can be manipulated at will."[42] This message, indeed, is the primary idea conveyed by female impersonation. Drag is a way of saying appearances can be deceiving, sex roles are irrelevant, gays are just as good as straights, not all who look like women *are* women, and not all who look straight are straight. People are people—whether they be gay or straight, male or female—regardless of appearances. As Newton says, "It seems self-evident that persons classified as 'men' would have to create artificially the image of a 'woman,' but of course 'women' have to create the image 'artificially' too."[43]

Female impersonation has a long history in the "legitimate" theater. In ancient Greece, Japan, China, and Great Britain women's roles were played by men and boys. (In Japan women were banned from the stage in 1628 on charges of prostitution; boys were banned from the stage in 1652. A similar ban in China began in the eighteenth century.)[44] Drag has also played a cohesive role in the gay subculture for centuries. According to Roger Baker, an early report of homosexual men in drag was written in England by Edward Ward in 1709, and similar accounts were common throughout the eighteenth century.[45] In more recent times the practice has been noted in the United States. In 1899 Joel S. Harris gave testimony regarding men in drag in New York City:

These men that congregate there—well, they act effeminately; most of them are painted and powdered; they are called Princess this and Lady So and So and the Duchess of Marlboro, and get up and sing as women, and dance; ape the female character, call each other sisters and take people out for immoral purposes.[46]

Drag shows in general and drag beauty contests in particular are festive events in the gay subculture. Beverly Stoeltje points out that festivals are "held within a community setting, expressing traditions meaningful to that community and [they are] produced by and for its members, not for outside consumption." She also says that festival time is different from normal time, that it is a time when usually deviant forms of behavior are tolerated (including reversal of male and female roles), and that "this transformation has often been described as . . . a negation of the social order."[47] In just such a way drag shows are a form of in-group entertainment built upon role reversal and calling into question the validity of the heterosexual social order.

Female impersonators adopt a wide variety of names to emphasize the images they wish to create. Names having an elegant or French sound, like Ramona Halston and DeAnne Devereaux, are common; so are comic (and often semierotic) names, like Kitty Litter and Eda Fucox. Sometimes the impersonators are aided in selecting their names by their "mothers." Many female impersonators consider themselves to be part of "mother-daughter" relationships. Rebecca Armstrong explains the relationship succinctly.

> I consider my mother, it would be Sonja Moritz. . . . 'Cause when I first started working in Indianapolis she did *everything* she possibly could to help me—gave me a place to stay so I wouldn't have to drive back and forth, you know, till I got my place. And gave me clothes when I needed it, and makeup tips. So to me *she* had to be *my* mother.
> It was usually somebody that's been around for a while, but sees somebody new that they think maybe had potential, or, you know, [they] just particularly like. And you kind of take them under your wings, say, "Now, you *do* this, and *don't* do that." You know, teach them the kind of the ropes, and stuff like that, and you know, it just kind of develops into like a mother—well like a mother telling her daughter, you know, something like that. It's real common.[48]

A typical drag show involves four or five female impersonators dancing and lip-syncing to records. (It is rare for a performer to sing, although until about 1960 live vocals were apparently more common than lip-syncing.) Sometimes shows include production numbers by most of the cast. One performer usually serves as the announcer, although this role may also be filled by the disk jockey or someone else. Guest performers frequently appear in the shows. Each impersonator generally does one number, after which another performer appears. After each cast member has performed once, each does a second number, and later a third. On occasion each impersonator will do several songs before the next performer appears to do her set. The show usually lasts an hour to an hour and a half.

The ultimate drag show is the drag beauty pageant. These events are taken quite seriously. The contestants must go through talent, evening gown, and swimsuit competitions, as well as interviews with the contest judges. From local pageants, winners progress to state and regional competitions. The winners of these pageants, in turn, vie for the titles of Miss Gay America and Miss Gay U.S.A. Apparently there is not yet a Miss Gay Universe pageant.

Outside the setting of the drag show, female impersonators often play the role of the trickster. Barbara Kirshenblatt-Gimblett, writing about the narratives of immigrants, says that "the protagonists of [immigrants'] stories are . . . sometimes tricksters, who are considered to be without culture because they are between cultures. What they know from the Old Country they cannot use and what they need in order to make it in America, they do not yet know."[49] Female impersonators enjoy a somewhat different status. Being a part of two cultures—gay and straight—they can use aspects of one to invert the value system of the other, which often results in stories in which gays can triumph over straights.

In the following narrative, Darla Lee tells of an encounter with a policeman.

I got stopped by the police one night, and he looked in the car—me
and Shelly Adams, at the old Omni, we came up in drag, and I picked up
a guy, and we went to my apartment, and coming back, he had a fifth of
vodka. And I wasn't paying any attention, and I picked it up and took a
big swig out of it, and about that time the police came around the corner.
And they followed us back in front of the bar, and he looked in and he
said, "Could I see your I.D., ma'am?" So I got it out of my purse and gave
it to him. And he said, "*Sure* this is yours?"

"Yeah."

He said, "Well, will you get out the car? I want to run some tests." So
[laughs], so he made me touch my nose and all this stuff. And then he
said, "You know you shouldn't be drinking and driving."

And I said, "Yes, I know, but I couldn't help myself."

And he said, "Well, is there anybody in there that can drive you home?"

I told him yes, that's why I'd came back, so my friend could drive me
home. And so I went in and got Shelly, and Shelly was drunker than I
was. She was running around with her skirt up above her crotch, and her
boobs a-hanging out. So we walked out and the police just kind of
looked. So we went home.

But I never will forget that night, the way that poor old cop looked
when he saw my driver's license.[50]

Not only did Darla have the policeman fooled as to her sex, she also tricked him
out of giving her a ticket or arresting her by telling him that she had come back
to have Shelly drive her home. Although this narrative deals with a potential
conflict, its primary function is cohesive, since in it Darla outwits a straight
authority figure.

Here is another story Darla tells about making a man believe that what he saw
was what he wanted it to be.

There was one other time. Me and Rebecca and Prunella Dalrymple
were going to Indianapolis. And we were just painted from the neck up.
And it was summer out. And this guy drove by us and he kept looking at
us. We kept yelling at him. And we slowed down some, and he asked us
where we was going. And we told him we was going to Indianapolis. And
he said, "Well, one of you want to ride with me?" And 'bout that time Rebecca stuck her leg up in the window and said, "Yes, I will!" And this [was]
when she had all her hair on her legs. And that guy looked, and I mean
he was down that road slicker 'n shit.

But we did. We laughed about it all the way up there.[51]

It is interesting to compare this text with Rebecca's version of the story.

One time me and Prunella and Darla were going to Indianapolis for a
show, and I had a pair—it was real hot and I had a pair of cut-offs on. I
hadn't started shaving my legs yet. And this guy kept passing us, and
waving, slowing down. We'd pass him, you know. 'Cause all he could see

was from here [indicates chest] on. And we finally get up to him at a stop light and he says, "I want to take the middle one with me!" And that was *me*. And *I* was going to *go!* Shit, I don't care.

Then he saw the hair on my legs and he . . . I bet he was in Indianapolis in the next five minutes, he went out that fast. [52]

The details of these two stories are the same, but Rebecca, quite naturally, focuses a little more heavily upon herself than Darla does.

Sometimes the deception is carried even further, as the next two examples illustrate. The first was told by Rebecca, the second by Sabrina Focks.

One time me and my roommate went out. We decided we was going to get painted up and go out. So we went out and hit *all* the *straight* places, you know, where the high school kids hang out and stuff. These two guys picked us up. Well, he knew what *she* was; you know, he was bisexual, and he didn't care. But the other one that picked *me* up thought I was *real*. And we got home, and things started to happen, and he finally realized that I was a man, and it freaked him out. [Laughter.] I loved that. [53]

One little Wednesday, long ago and far away, we got through with the show. I didn't meet a man at the bar, and it was time to go. On my way home this black man drove by in a big brown Thunderbird. He goes around the block again, and he's cruising me. He stops the car and asks if I need a ride. I said no thanks, that I didn't have to walk far. He said he didn't think it was safe for a lady to be walking the streets late at night. So I thought, "What the fuck. I'll get in."

So we rode home. I don't know what all he told me—we were just making small talk. After we got to the parking lot of my apartment he said he thought he should see me to the door. So I thought, "All right." So after we got to the door he asked if he could come inside, so I said sure.

So we sat down on the couch and started to make out. So one thing led to another and we started to go to the bedroom.

We just got in the bedroom, kind of right inside the doorway, and he proceeds to slip his hand down inside my bodysuit, and he pulls out my falsie. And he said, "Oh, my God!" He goes, "You only have one breast." So then he reaches in the other side and he pulls the other one out. So I don't know why, but for some reason he still thought I was a woman and I'd had a double mastectomy. So he naturally at this point—I don't know exactly what he thought, but I don't think he knew what he was getting into. He thought I was a real woman.

I think one thing's very important: he still hadn't backed away from me yet; he's still holding me close, kissing me. And he proceeded to let his hand drift farther below. Well, of course, by the time he got down there, as much necking as there was going on, there was quite a bulge down there, and that was the point he realized I was a man and [he] kind of freaked out.

Well, he started saying, "Wait a minute, wait a minute. I'm not into this."

And I pointed out to him that he still had an erection, and I said, "Well it didn't bother you that much or you'd've lost your erection very quickly." So I started pulling him into bed and pulled him down on top of me—oh, my God! You want me to go *on*? So he's kissing me. I started pulling clothes off him and he started getting into it at this point.

The weird thing is, until he got to the falsies, I was feeling *fish!*[54]

In these two instances the men were convinced that the narrators were women; when the first found out that his companion was male, "he freaked"; the second, however, succumbed to the trickster's charms.

The trickster in drag nonpareil is Ramona Halston. The following is her account of her visit to a straight bar in Bloomington.

Joe: What about the thing at the Ramada Inn? Tell me about that.

Ramona: The reason it was decided that I was going to go was—the week before—let's see, me and a few of my friends, we just went out on a Sunday night to have some drinks, and the deejay is a friend of mine. And he's straight, but he has come in to see one or two of the shows. But I knew him from another bar; he was deejay there. And they just—in the middle of a song I hear an announcement that Ramona Halston, a New York *Cosmopolitan* and *Vogue* model would be at the Ramada Inn, Diamond Lil's at the Ramada Inn the next Sunday night.

And I just thought—it didn't really hit me who they'd said. I thought, oh—I just looked at [my roommate] and thought, "A *model* is going to be *here?*" [Laughter.] And she's looking at me like [sharp intake of breath], "Ramona! [Narrator used his real name.] What are they saying?" [Laughs.] You know. And it took a minute for it to sink in, and then I ran to [the deejay] and I just, you know, "*What* are you talking about?" And he said, "You've been announced. You've got to be here."

So, I was very nervous. [Laughs.] I don't know. I felt like—I felt real good about it. It went really good. When we went in, we went in and sat down, and the waitress came over with a big silver tray and leaned down and asked me if I was, "Excuse me, are you Miss Halston?" And I [said], "Um, yes." [Laughs.] And she said, "Well, um, I have this note for you." And so it was laying on this silver tray. I took it, and it just said, I think it said something like, it said, "Miss Halston, we want to welcome you to the Ramada Inn," and it was signed, "The Manager of Diamond Lil's." And then she said, "And," you know, "the first round of drinks for you and all your friends are on the house."

So, and then, as the night went on, everybody was, I don't know whether—the talk kind of went through the crowd that this was a model, and people were sending me drinks and sending little notes, you know, telling how happy they were I was in Bloomington, and stuff like guys flirting around and stuff. And it was scary. [Laughter.][55]

For a man to pass as a woman is an accomplishment; for him to pass as a female fashion model is a major achievement.

In all of these stories, the narrators focus on their ability to be mistaken for women. They view female impersonation as an art, and they are proud of their expertise. The humor in most of the stories turns on the victims' discovery that they have been duped. The embarrassment of the men involved, being confronted with their error, doubles the humor resulting from their initial ignorance. As Esther Newton says, "Beating women at the glamour game is a feat valued by all female impersonators and by many homosexuals in general."[56] Success in such endeavors is a victory to be shared with other members of the subculture. The sense of achievement reinforces group solidarity.

Gays' responses to drag vary. As one person put it, female impersonators are "neither fish nor fowl," making a pun on the gay word *fish* and also on the words *fowl* and *foul*. Rebecca Armstrong gives a somewhat bitter summary of the reactions she has encountered: "Gay men don't want us because we look real, and straight men don't want us because we aren't real."[57] Within the subculture female impersonators are accepted and enjoyed while giving shows. On an individual basis most of them are also quite popular, but many gays feel that drag is misogynistic and therefore divisive at a time when there is a great need for unity among lesbians and gay men. (Interestingly, many of the most ardent fans of the drag shows are lesbians. Some have told the performers that they wish the impersonators would be more butch in drag, in other words, impersonating dykes.)

Although doing drag is usually seen as an expression of effeminacy, it is in fact an assertive, perhaps even aggressive, act. Female impersonators can use their effeminacy as a means of flouting standard values. A man in drag is "on stage," asserting his personality (and his effeminacy) as surely as is the man playing a macho role. He is saying, "Look; here I am. This is me, and you can't get away from me. *Look* at me. I'm beautiful. *Admire* in me the stereotypes you despise in gay men."[58] An extreme example of the aggression expressed by drag is gender-fuck drag, in which the performers are in full drag (makeup, gowns, wigs, heels, jewelry) but also have beards or mustaches.

From straight audiences, drag either requires a suspension of disbelief or demands a questioning of long-held values. Although female impersonators may be ridiculed by some, they force all but the most impervious viewers to question the validity of sex-role stereotypes. For some, of course, drag merely reinforces such stereotypes, but the person exposed to drag in its subcultural context will also be exposed to other aspects of homosexuality. It would be extremely difficult to enter a gay bar and watch a drag show without noticing that the men present contradict more stereotypes than they fit.

In fostering cohesion gay folklore conveys many messages. The commonality of experience enables members of the subculture to laugh at themselves; to ridicule the straight world and conventional values; to understand that various fears, although by no means groundless, are normal and can be faced and overcome; to see themselves as good, valuable members of society rather than degenerate perverts; and to know that they are not alone in their predicament, for their gay brothers can help them cope with whatever problems they encounter. As Maurice Leznoff and William A. Westley sum it up, "The gossip about sex, the adoption and exaggeration of feminine behavior, and the affectation of speech, represent a way of affirming that homosexuality is frankly accepted and has the collective support of the group."[59] The resulting cohesion helps gay people reach levels three through five in the acculturation process (association with the subculture, attaining cultural competence, and serving as models for other newcomers).

Cohesion is also partly a reaction to conflict. Shared pressures from society cause gays to unite against a common enemy, an interaction that is evident in the folklore gay men use in expressing and coping with conflict.

❧ 4

Better Blatant than Latent

CONFLICT AND THE GAY SUBCULTURE

A PERSON BECOMING PART of a stigmatized subculture must face and learn to deal with conflict with the larger culture. Generally he or she will also encounter intrasubcultural conflict. Such conflict is particularly evident in the gay subculture. Gays experience conflict with the straight world because of society's lack of tolerance of homosexuality. Racism, misogyny (including a widespread dislike of lesbians), and other prejudices carry over into the gay world from the larger culture. These attitudes are widely expressed in gay folklore, often veiled as humor. Among gay men this covert conflict is intensified because of a strong need to feel superior to some group of people. Popularly viewed as the lowest of the low, gays respond by asserting that there are people inferior even to them. These groups—especially women, blacks, and ethnic peoples—thus become a safe and easy target for gays' suppressed anger. A reluctance to accept female impersonators and flaming queens is also common in the subculture, since many gays feel that such people are "politically incorrect," reinforcing straights' stereotypes of gays and thereby hindering the cause of gay liberation.

By serving as a pressure valve, a means of conveying veiled insults, and a method of confronting and expressing prejudices, folklore becomes a way of coping with the tension that results from these conflicts. Folklore also functions as a defense mechanism, affirming the dignity of gay people in spite of the prevailing feeling in the straight world that gays are, at best, sick.

Much of the tension gay people must cope with arises from the heterosexual culture's categorizing them as abnormal. This pressure is intensified by the reprobation many churches reserve for gays and by federal, state, and local laws that deny them many of the civil rights and protections guaranteed to all other citizens of the United States.[1]

This stigmatization and discrimination have made it necessary for many homosexual people to conceal their sexual orientation. Having grown up in a straight culture, gays find that the technique of "passing" comes easily. The psychological cost of this process, however, is high, since it puts one into conflict with himself. On the other hand, as William H. Martineau has pointed out, "conflict is not always dysfunctional for the system; it does not necessarily lead to disintegration."[2] Indeed, conflict between the gay and straight cultures strengthens the cohesion among gays. Without pressure from outside the community it is quite likely that the gay subculture would cease to exist.

Franz Boas said that folklore mirrors culture; Ruth Benedict added that folklore also *distorts* culture. Writing about a gay bar in the western United States, Kenneth E. Read expresses the same ideas, using Jean Genet's image of a hall of mirrors in which everything is reflected but distorted. He points out that behaviors exhibited by gay men

are essentially ritual enactments of heterosexual myths of homosexuals, using deliberate distortions to disvalue the "truth" of the myths and, through a process of refractions, thereby communicating and identifying the homosexual's existential experience of inclusion and exclusion.[3]

Gays intentionally distort their culture *and* straight culture, showing straight people what they expect to see, insulting them without their awareness. The folklore arising from conflict situations masks the bitterness that has grown out of the tension caused by oppression.

When gays use their folklore to cope with such pressures, it serves to invalidate the straight world. In doing so, it validates the gay culture.[4] The flouting of heterosexual values at once strengthens and affirms the gay subculture and mocks and questions the values of the larger heterosexual culture. It is this defiance that is the essence of much gay folklore.

Read interprets gay defiance of straight values as " 'rites of intensification' . . . [that] turn the stigmatization into a 'virtue.' "[5] In this way gays can view the heterosexual world as ridiculous and nonthreatening.

One source of conflict with the straight society is the stereotypes many heterosexual people hold about gays. Stereotypes serve as a form of shorthand for communicating with oneself and with others. They also represent, according to Walter Lippmann,

the guarantee of our self-respect; . . . the projection upon the world of our own sense of our own value, our own position and our own rights. The stereotypes are, therefore, highly charged with the feelings that are attached to them. They are the fortress of our tradition, and behind its defenses we can continue to feel ourselves safe in the position we occupy.[6]

Lippmann goes on to point out that our perception of situations is strongly shaped by the stereotypes we hold; we tend to ignore information contrary to our point of view.[7] As he explains,

Since my moral system rests on my accepted version of the facts, he who denies either my moral judgments or my version of the facts, is to me perverse, alien, dangerous. How shall I account for him? The opponent has always to be explained, and the last explanation that we ever look for is that he sees a different set of facts. Such an explanation we avoid, because it saps the very foundation of our own assurance that we have seen life steadily and seen it whole. It is only when we are in the habit of recognizing our opinions as a partial experience seen through our stereotypes that we become truly tolerant of an opponent. Without that habit, we believe in the absolutism of our own vision, and consequently in the treacherous character of all opposition. For while men are willing to admit that there are two sides to a "question," they do not believe that there are two sides to what they regard as a "fact." And they never do believe it until after long critical education, they are fully conscious of how second-hand and subjective is their apprehension of the social data.[8]

The strongly held stereotypes of gays support Lippmann's argument. The perseverance of stereotypes despite frequent refutation by psychologists, sociologists, and other researchers underscores the tenacity of traditional attitudes, mind-sets that are firmly resistant to change even in the light of overwhelming scientific evidence. A limited familiarity breeds contempt, which can be overcome only through understanding.

Many negative stereotypes are very effective because they appeal to basic fears. The stereotype of the effeminate gay male not only contains a value judgment that holds that nonmasculine men are weak, ineffective, and deviant; it also appeals to the insecurity many men have about their own sexuality. When confronted with men who experience their sexuality differently from the way one expresses his own, a man is likely to be challenged to question his sexual values. Either he reaffirms the code of behavior he has long held or he faces the frightening possibility that those whom society calls deviant may not be so bad after all.

Emotionally laden words are often used to increase the impact of negative stereotypes. Anita Bryant's Save Our Children campaign in 1977 and the Rev. Jerry Falwell's Moral Majority have, in their verbal attacks on gay people, stressed the threat they believe gays pose to homes, families, and children. (As John Boswell points out, "no charge against a minority seems to be more damaging than the claim that they pose a threat of some sort to the children of the majority."[9])

In 1977, Anita Bryant and her then-husband Bob Green launched a campaign to repeal a gay-rights ordinance in Dade County, Florida. Although they were successful in their attempt, the publicity they attracted and the pressure they exerted upon the gay community resulted in a strengthened and better organized gay liberation movement. The same results occurred after the Rev. Jerry Falwell's establishment in 1979 of his ultraconservative and ultrafundamentalist-Christian Moral Majority. Falwell's organization is dedicated to maintaining and strengthening "Christian" values, ferreting out gay people, outlawing abortion, and legalizing prayer in public schools.

The gay community quickly responded to the Moral Majority with buttons, banners, bumper stickers, and tee shirts proclaiming, "The Moral Majority is neither," "Oral Majority" (a pun on oral sex), and "Immoral Minority." Bryant's crusade also sparked gays' creativity. Given Bryant's background as a spokesperson for the Florida citrus industry and punning on the word *fruit* as a synonym for *gay,* gay people soon began using the slogan "Suck a fruit for Anita." They based another slogan on the citrus industry's motto, changing it from "A day without orange juice is like a day without sunshine" to "A day without human rights is like a day without sunshine."

Few words in English carry stronger positive connotations for most people than *home, family,* and *children.* Including these terms in stereotypes of gays as immoral and mentally ill greatly increases the implied threat. The two movements cited grew out of fundamentalist Christian organizations, but their psychologically loaded stereotypes present homosexuality as a threat to cultural values that extends far beyond such groups' Judeo-Christian roots. Thus, by combining psycholinguistic attacks with stereotypes, members of the straight culture have waged a strong verbal battle against the gay subculture.

One of the major responses of gay men to conflict with straights is expressed in terms of fear: fear of being attacked, fear of rape, fear of one's homosexuality being discovered, fear of losing one's job. These fears are reflected in folklore. Ramona Halston's narrative about being abducted, quoted in the last chapter, is a good example of a cautionary tale. In the story Ramona relates a frightening experience of being assaulted, a situation that many gay men fear. Her tale warns listeners that danger is real, and anyone can be confronted by it.

Another example is the following legend, probably the most common one in current circulation in the gay community.

> I just thought of one: story about the gay who went into a glory hole— that is a john which has a hole cut in the partition in the crappers, OK?— and he stuck his cock through the hole and was well massaged by the person on the other side, who then stuck a hatpin through his cock, preventing his exit from the hole.
>
> That I find not a joke. It's too painful. Therefore it's a legend. It may be true; God knows. It's a horrible concept. . . .
>
> I've heard it reported all over every place. The last I heard it reported was in a highway rest stop in Michigan. But I heard it in fifteen different guises from New York to Indianapolis.[10]

Frequenting the tearooms—public restrooms that serve as places for homosexual encounters—and using the glory holes for anonymous sex are acts that carry with them an excitement enhanced by the anonymity *and* the possibility of being discovered. Such meetings are also influenced by an undercurrent of uncertainty. Not knowing one's sexual partner—often not even knowing what he looks like—may increase the excitement, but it carries with it a nagging doubt as well. The potential for danger is always present: one might encounter a homophobic straight person, as the attacker in this example is often assumed to be. Unspoken though the fear may be, it is a real fear, and it is verbalized in narratives such as this one.

R. D. Fenwick reports another legend, a story that deals with the near discovery of a man's homosexuality (or at least his penchant for extranormal sexual interests).

> **The story may be apocryphal, but it's making the rounds in Chicago. An executive was wearing one of these inventions ["a padlocked leather belt around the waist and a strap between the legs that's attached to a six-inch dildo, or 'butt plug' "] when, at his office, he was suddenly stricken with diarrhea. Unable to locate his "master," who had the key, our hero had to send his secretary to the building maintenance department for a pair of tin-snips.** [11]

This poor man was almost caught, and many homosexual people are afraid that their secret will likewise be discovered. This legend, like the glory hole narrative, warns listeners to be careful, to be discreet, lest their fears be actualized.

Within the gay community, violation of subcultural behavior codes is also a source of conflict. When gay men are cruising one another, the revelation of one's surname and more than minimal personal information is sometimes considered an affront since it carries an implied request for similar details from the potential partner.

Sometimes mistakes of this sort can be overlooked, just as a minor social gaffe such as using the wrong piece of silverware at a formal dinner may be taken as a sign of a lack of proper training, but rarely would it cause offense. On the other hand, some violations are taken as affronts. For example, in some cities, acceptance of an invitation to dance is considered to be acceptance of a proposition as well. A person unaware of this convention and refusing the proposition after having accepted the invitation would be considered rude at best.

The broadest and most obvious group of conflict situations is evident in the many we-they dichotomies present both within the subculture and between the gay and straight communities. As members of a stigmatized subculture, gay people find themselves in a category distinct from the much larger heterosexual culture. This gay-straight opposition is maintained by both groups and is expressed through jokes and stereotypes. Gays' mistrust of and disdain for straights can be seen in the epithet "filthy breeders" as well as in such comments as, "I think it's very important to have straight people," a statement that seems positive on the surface; however, it carries an implied "but . . . ."[12]

The gay-straight conflict, although it encompasses many emotional issues, boils down to a misogynistic stereotype long supported by Western societies. Women are seen as weak and ineffectual; gay men are assumed to be effeminate, thus weak and ineffectual and therefore like women. Gay men are bad because they try to be like women; at least women cannot help being female.

Gay men have not worked to attain their masculine status. As Esther Newton points out, "The dichotomy appears in American culture as rooted in 'nature.' One can just *be* a woman; it is a passive state. But one must *achieve* manhood."[13] This view of homosexuality has given rise to one of the most common lines in the gay subculture. When a gay man feels that his masculinity has been impugned by a straight male, the traditional retort is, "Honey, I'm more man than you'll ever *be* and more woman than you'll ever get."[14] With these few words the gay man has asserted his masculinity (and his androgyny), expressed pride in his homosexuality, and psychologically castrated his opponent.

As this line reminds us, gay men *are* men and as such enjoy privileges traditionally allowed men in most cultures. Many of the jokes told in our society, including a large number of those told by gays, are misogynistic.[15] In these jokes (told by gay and straight men alike) we see a set of shared attitudes: women are seen as ignorant, repulsive, useless (except for sex), and incomplete without a man. The following examples will illustrate this point.

> **Tarzan is swinging through the jungle and meets Jane. He says [deep voice]: "Me Tarzan. What *your* name?" [Coy, high voice, rising inflection]: "Jane." [Tarzan voice:] "What your *whole* name?" [Jane voice:] "Cunt."**

In this joke, women, through Jane, are depicted as being ignorant, capable of mistaking *whole* for *hole*. They are reduced to a single physical feature, the vagina, and are thus viewed as sex objects. And, since it is *Jane's* stupidity that creates the joke, women are presented as being preoccupied with sex. Here is another example:

> **Do you know what a gynecologist is?**
> **A person who spreads old wives' tails.**

The pun on "old wives' tales" in this joke is the source of humor, at the expense of bringing women once again down to the level of being mere objects. In a similar vein, the next example not only treats women as objects, it also compares them to a convenience item (almost like "fast food").

> **Why are women's cunts and assholes so close together?**
> **So when they get drunk you can carry them home like a six-pack [of beer].**

The next step down is to rob women of their humanity altogether.

> **How many animals can you get into a pair of pantyhose?**
> **Thirteen: ten piggies, two calves, and one pussy.[16]**

Since women can be reduced to subhuman status in the subcultural psyche, it becomes easy to regard them as repulsive, as in the following example.

Why do women have legs?
Because if they didn't they'd leave sticky trails like slugs.

Here again women are equated with animals, in this case slimy nocturnal creatures most people find extremely unattractive.

From being repulsive to being worthless is a small move. If something is so undesirable (women, in these jokes), is there any reason to use it at all? The jokes say no.

Why do they put weathercocks on buildings?
Because the wind would blow right through a cunt.[17]

Finally, women are considered to be incomplete without men.

What do dildos and soybeans have in common?
They're both meat substitutes.

What do you call a truckload of dildos?
Toys for twats.

These two jokes imply that women need penises, a form of penis-envy attributed to women by men. Since a dildo is a substitute for the "real thing," women who use them are seen as inferior. The implication here is that for a woman to be as good as a man she would have to have a penis. (And, by extension, one *could* interpret the ultimate message of the joke to be that the best type of sexual relationship is that available only between men.)

Of women Rebecca Armstrong says, "They're all right to look at."[18] This statement was delivered in a campy manner, in much the same way one would say, "Some of my best friends are." But as with the jokes, this line conveys a subtle message of misogyny. Why is this attitude so common in the gay subculture? The primary reason is its prevalence in the straight culture. In addition, Ramona Halston points out that men feel that they can compete with men, but not with women.[19] Women pose a threat.

Misogyny carries over into the we-they dichotomy of lesbian and gay male. The common stereotype of dykes (as opposed to lesbians) held by many straights is also held by a lot of gay men. As John Herrick summarizes it, "I like lesbians; I can't stand dykes. . . . The dyke is tough, raucous, highly emotional, apt to pick fights and cause disturbances."[20] Dykes are also seen as fat, or at least stocky, and extremely butch. This view is evident in the following jokes.

Do you know what the difference between a killer whale and a bull dyke is?
About fifty pounds and a flannel shirt.

This example expresses the stereotype succinctly. The next joke includes a reference to another attribute of the stereotypical dyke: she rides a motorcycle.

> Do you know how to tell a really butch dyke when you see one?
> She has a kick-starter on her vibrator.

Here once again is the implication that women are inferior to men since they do not have penises.

The image of the overly aggressive dyke is combined with a blatant indelicacy in another joke.

> Do you know how to tell a really butch dyke?
> She rolls her own tampons.

Not only is this woman seen as inappropriately masculine (by analogy to rolling one's own cigarettes); she is also portrayed as disgusting, putting a tampon to her mouth. And, since men have no need of tampons, the dyke, despite the homosexuality she shares with gay men, joins other women in being considered useless.

Lesbians do not have to be dykes to be a subject for gay ridicule.

> How many lesbians does it take to screw in a light bulb?
> None. Lesbians don't screw.

Since they "don't screw," lesbians obviously cannot enjoy sexual relations as much as gay men (or straight men and women).

Racism is another manifestation of conflict. Although most gays deny being bigoted, racist jokes are common in the subculture, largely because of the predominance of this type of humor and many of the same jokes in the straight culture. The jokes, like misogynistic humor, are based on stereotypes and reveal attitudes shared by straight and gay white men. Blacks are depicted in the jokes as stupid, unclean, and fond of watermelon. The following is a typical racist joke.

> Janie and Liza are walking down the street and they look up and see this big, fat black woman sitting up on a balcony. She's got her skirt way up around her waist and she's not wearing any underwear, and she's eating a big slice of watermelon. So Janie yells up, "Say, sister! Say, you all nice and cool up there with yo' skirt pulled up around yo' waist?" And she said, "Well, I ain't very cool, but it sho' do keep the flies off my watermelon."

Some straight white men would consider a black woman's vagina foul and filthy. To many gay men *any* vagina would seem foul and filthy, as well as useless. This attitude is clear in both the previous joke and the following example.

> What's the difference between a bowling ball and a nigger cunt?
> You can eat a bowling ball if you have to.

To describe a bowling ball as edible in contrast to a "nigger cunt" is a clear statement of disgust at the thought of a black woman's genitalia.

The jokes also portray blacks as promiscuous and preoccupied with sex (an interesting projection, since the same stereotype is held by straights about gays):

> Janie and Liza were walking down the beach, and they saw two other sisters lying on the beach. They walked up to them and Janie said, "Say, sisters, say what you doin' lyin' here with yo' hair all braided and pomaded and tryin' to look like Injuns?"
> And one of them said, "There must be some mistake. I'm a Navajo and she's an Arapaho."
> And Janie said, "Well ain't that a coincidence! I'm a Toledo 'ho' and she's a Chicago 'ho'."

Here Janie and Liza are depicted as being so obsessed with sex that they are ignorant of everything else. They hear "Navajo" and "Arapaho" as "Nava [w]ho[re]" and "Arapa [w]ho[re]."

The following joke is also based on the stereotype of blacks' sexual pre-occupation.

> Janie and Liza go to confession on Christmas Eve, and when they come out of the confessionals Janie says, "Law', I sho' does feel better. Say, what you get, sister?"
> And Liza says, "I gots to do the stations."
> And Janie says, "Well, I does too. Say, ain't no point in us bof doin' all of 'em. Say, why don't we split 'em up. You take the po-lice stations and I'll take the fire stations."

In this joke the women confuse the penance of doing the Stations of the Cross with "doing" (having sexual relations with the staffs of) the police and fire stations.

The racist element in gay humor can be ascribed partly to the deep-seated need most people feel to be better than someone else. Just as Hoosiers tell Kentuckian jokes, Georgians tell jokes about Alabamians, who in turn put down Mississippians, who refer to "those dumb Arkansawyers," who along with people throughout the country tell Polish jokes. So too do homosexual people, considered by many to be the underside of the dregs of society, feel a need to be better than someone, anyone. Seeing themselves as "sexual niggers," white gays can consider themselves socially and intellectually better than blacks—straight or gay.

Interestingly, many of those who frequently tell racist jokes have close black friends. The racism present in the humor is apparently a mental construct that allows an emotional sense of superiority that for the most part does not manifest itself in one's social practices. The psychological expressions of bigotry are seldom realized in one's relationships.

The expression of misogynistic and racist humor in the gay male community is ironic in that the oppressed have become the oppressors. Lesbians and gay men share the stigma of homosexuality. Even so, attitudes instilled and nurtured in white gay men during their heterosexual enculturation are deeply rooted and tenacious.

Blacks are not the only ethnic group subjected to jokes told by gays. Chief among others are Jews and Poles. Jews are a special case. They may be depicted as stupid, but it is a stupidity masking a clever, cunning mind. The proud, doting mother figures prominently in jokes about Jews, and the stereotype of the penny-pinching Jew is not ignored. The joke about the Greek, the Italian, and the Jew who find a magic lamp, discussed in chapter 2, is interesting in that it deals explicitly with stereotypes. Although the stereotypes of the pasta-loving Italian and the money-conscious Jew are verbalized in the joke, that of the Greek's preference for anal intercourse is only implied. Many straight people would fail to comprehend the reference to the Greek's presumed predisposition.

The stereotype of the Jewish mother who wants her sons to enter the professions and her daughters to marry professional men is evident in the following two jokes.

A Jewish woman is walking down the street with her two sons and she meets a friend of hers who asks, "So, how old are your children?"
She says, "The doctor's five and the lawyer's three."

Two Jewish women are talking on the phone and one says, "Golda, today I got good news and bad news."
And the other one says, "Oh, My God, Sophie! What's the bad news?"
"Well, Golda, today my son calls me, he tells me he's queer."
"Oh, Sophie, that is bad news. What's the good news?"
"He's married a doctor."

The first example shows the Jewish mother's tendency (according to the stereotype) to dominate and decide the futures of her children, and the second points out that even though she may not always be successful, she will try to direct the situation to her advantage. Her son's homosexuality is compensated for by his "marriage" to a doctor. There is the implication, however, that the son has for his mother been transformed into a daughter. For this reason the joke becomes for gays a statement of the Jewish mother's ignorance (thinking that "marrying" a doctor will overcome the stigma attached to her son's homosexuality—and by extension attached to her) rather than praise of her tolerance.

Poles and "Polacks" (Polish Americans) have come to epitomize stupidity and uncleanliness in American humor. The jokes told by gay men are no exception. Once again misogyny is a strong element in the jokes. The Poles are depicted as being almost willfully ignorant; they are confronted with situations that cause them to respond in ways that indicate a lack of intelligence difficult to comprehend.

A Polish teenager told her mother, "I think I'm pregnant."
Her mother said, "Are you sure it's yours?"

Did you hear about the Polish woman who had an abortion?
She wasn't sure the baby was hers.

A pregnant woman could conceivably not know the identity of her baby's father, but she would have to be totally non compos mentis not to know who the mother was.

If Polish women are at best naïve regarding sex and reproduction, then they must also be unversed in hygiene.

What do Polish women and hockey players have in common?
They both change pads after the fourth period.

What do Polish women and basketball players have in common?
They both shower after the fourth period.

Do you know how to tell when a Polish woman is having her period?
She's only wearing one bobby sock.

Did you hear about the deadly disease going around in Poland?
Toxic Sock Syndrome.

The thought of a woman who does not clean herself after having a period is—to most men—repugnant. The notion of using a sock for a maxipad, although it is better than not changing pads at all, is not much more appealing.

As with the previous Polish jokes, the next example is misogynistic; it also addresses the gay male-lesbian conflict.

Did you hear about the Polish lesbian?
She traded her menstrual cycle in for a Suzuki.[21]

Not only is the woman a stereotypically stupid Pole, she is also a stereotypical dyke, riding a motorcycle.

By combining ethnic slurs with misogyny, these jokes present *all* women and members of various other groups as repulsive, vulgar, and ignorant. The implication is that the subjects of the jokes are being compared with the members of the teller's group, who do not exhibit such negative traits.

Straight women who spend large portions of their time with gay men are the source of another form of conflict in the subculture. The tension is expressed only occasionally, as in the names used in referring to these women—fag hags and fruit flies—but it is present nevertheless.

Carol A. B. Warren identifies three roles for women among gay men: the decorative, the surrogate (through which gay men can vicariously enjoy glamour in public or semipublic situations without going in drag), and the functional (whereby the woman provides a mask for the gay male, allowing him to pass as straight).[22] The motivations of these women are as varied as the women themselves. Warren suggests that many of the women are avoiding the stigma attached in our society to "older, divorced heterosexual women."[23] Charles Silverstein and Edmund White point out that straight women can associate with gay men without being confronted with sexual expectations, thus having comfortable, nonthreatening relationships with males.[24]

Interestingly, although fag hags do not constitute a group, they are *perceived* by gay men as being a group. They are a sort of parasitic phenomenon; they could not exist without the subculture, although the subculture would certainly exist without them. They exist only because gays allow them to. When asked where fag hags fit in in relation to the subculture, Michael Monroe said, "I don't think they fit in; I think they're acolytes." In other words, they are the community's ladies in waiting (attendant upon the queens). Bob Schultz said, "Fag hags aren't important to the gay community—but then, no one is."[25]

Marc Henderson gives a good description of the fag hag's role.

A fag hag, in the circles that I ran around in, was a woman who preferred the company of gay men. Now . . . their internal motivations may be divisible into two or more groups. In my set nobody *cared* what their motivations were. Nobody really cared what their feelings were about anything. A fag hag was a woman who—she was a doll. You could dress her up, and tart up her face, and go with her when she bought clothes, and choose her jewelry for her, and her makeup, and her perfume, and teach her to dance, and get her into gay bars, and feel real virtuous and real feminist for running her past the person at the door who was supposed to keep women out of the bar.

She was someone to talk to and cry on her shoulder—and God forbid she should cry on yours. She was somebody to get drunk. . . . She usually had to have a real resilient sense of humor in order to deal with all the antifemale humor that came her way. She had to have a self-deprecating kind of humor because she would meet with a lot of vicious insults thinly disguised as comic conversation. She was a pet straight person on whom to take out some of the aggressions of being stigmatized.

Now all of these aspects that I'm talking about are the way that *groups* of gay men related to fag hags. Now it was possible to develop an individual friendship with these women on a one-to-one basis. I saw that happen sometimes. *I* never made friends with any of them who were in our set, because I didn't have any use for these people.

. . . I did know people who got genuine enjoyment and who gave genuine enjoyment cruising together with women. Now that sometimes was something that people apparently had real fun with. You'd take a woman out to lunch and cruise all the men in the Mall. *That* maybe was not an unhealthy relationship.[26]

Viewed as a group but related to individually, fag hags enjoy a relatively amicable (albeit misogynistic and thus somewhat masochistic) relationship with the gay community, a degree of tolerance afforded few other outsiders.

In addition to the basic gay-straight dichotomy, several other we-they distinctions exist within the gay subculture. Merely naming something sets up the opposition defining the thing or person as part of a group—"what it is"—regardless of whether the category of "what it is not" has been labeled. Some people identify with the groups with which others associate them; other persons may be perceived as belonging to groups with which they do not identify. For example, some effeminate men are homosexual and consider themselves gay. Effeminate heterosexual men, however, are often assumed by others to be gay even though they are not.

A distinction is made between active and passive (inserter and insertee, respectively, during intercourse) that, although not necessarily a source of conflict, divides the gay world into two segments based on people's preferred sexual roles. The butch-fem dichotomy is similar, but it is based on the differences between masculine (or hypermasculine) and effeminate behavior. Thus even though these two categories seem similar, they are not the same. One may be butch and passive, for example.

The categories of butch and fem, on a visual level, are most obvious when one is dealing with drag and female impersonation. (There is not necessarily any correlation between female impersonation and effeminacy, however.) Female impersonators generally use the term *drag queen* in reference to themselves only around other impersonators and close friends. For them a drag queen is untalented; uses too much makeup, which is always poorly applied; wears tacky, unflattering clothes; and could never convince *anyone* that she is real. A female impersonator, on the other hand, is all that the drag queen is not: professional, glamorous, and believable. Most other gay men define only two categories: drag queens and those who do not do drag; they make no distinctions between female impersonators and drag queens. Many gays have negative feelings about drag, but those who criticize female impersonators for perpetuating stereotypes fail to remember that the Stonewall Riot was initiated by men in drag.[27]

Drag also represents conflict with the straight culture. It states that traditional sex roles are irrelevant. It is assertive, even aggressive. It forces the audience (whether a formal audience, watching a drag show, or an informal one comprising bystanders) to consider, at least temporarily, the possibility that men can be better women than *real* women.

Darla Lee tells the following story to illustrate this point.

Darla: When I bought my black boots, I asked her how big they were, you know, in sizes, because I really need a size eleven, but I can cram my feet into a size ten. And she said, "Size ten."

And I said, "Well, I'd like to see them." So she gave them to me and I said, "Well, do you think they'll stretch?"

She said, "No, they won't stretch."

And I said, "Do you care if I try them on?"

She said, "Well, they're *women's* boots."

And I said, "I know it. I just want to try them on."

She said, "Well, you can't here. You'll have to buy them."

And I said, "All right. If I buy them and they *don't* fit, can I get my money back?"

She said yes.

Anyway, I got them home and they fit, so I wore them out there. And I said, "Hey lady, remember me?" [Laughter.]

And she said, "Well, you look familiar."

And I said, "Well I was the guy that you said these boots wouldn't fit my feet, and see—they fit!"

Joe: Did you have on women's clothes? Did you have a wig . . . ?

Darla: Yes, it was before a show. I was all made. She liked to [have] *freaked!* I'm surprised they didn't put her in her grave, 'cause she was an old lady.[28]

In this situation, Darla was confronted by a woman appalled at the idea of a man wearing women's clothes. The woman's refusal to let her try on the boots and her disapproving attitude provoked Darla enough to make her return to the store in drag seeking revenge by shocking the salesclerk.

The opposite situation is related by Sabrina Focks, who describes an occasion in which she used drag to avoid the potential for conflict.

Young salesgirls, they just look at you kind of strange, like, "What he's looking at looks like it's his size." . . . *Older* salesladies are fantastic. I remember, one time I bought a pair of earrings, and the saleslady says, "Well, what are you going to do with them?"

And I said, "Well, I'm going to *wear* them!" [Laughter.]

She got so tickled. She goes, "You're *serious*, aren't you?"

And I said yes. So then I explained to her about the shows, and that's what I needed them for. And she came and saw one of the shows one night.[29]

By bridging the gap between the gay and straight cultures, Sabrina was able to enlighten at least one woman, whose attitudes toward gays presumably improved as a result of her exposure to drag.

Stereotypically effeminate behavior occurs much more often within the subculture than many gay men would like to admit. Generally it is either a transitory stage in the coming-out process or a humorous exaggeration of the behavior patterns straights expect from gays.[30] Michael Monroe describes his feelings about flaming queens in the following excerpt.

Based on my view of my own evolving life-style, I think that maybe being a flaming queen is an early episode in the coming-out cycle. It is kind of an affirmation of this queerness. It's a chip on the shoulder to me; it's sort of a chip-on-the-shoulder attitude. But it seems to me that it is like an overreaction to the previous years of suppression of all those feelings that were hidden away because they were gay. Now they're being trotted out because they're associated with being homosexual. . . .

. . . I always thought *I* was a flaming queen. And I think I must have been for a while. . . . I remember learning—when I first came out in '71—learning all the flamboyant gestures that gay people were using. And I quickly got a reputation for having a sharp wit and a sharper tongue. And I expect I was loud at that time, and I wish I had some way to go back and objectively review that time of my life, because it's something that I can't stomach now. I think it's the most inappropriate public display, simply because it's offensive to people—and unnecessarily offensive. I don't mind a good political statement that's offensive, but I don't consider most of that to be of the caliber to be considered an artistic political statement. I think it's just bad manners to foist oneself on the public that way.[31]

Marc Henderson has a somewhat different point of view.

On Tuesdays and Thursdays and Saturdays I *adore* [flaming queens]; they take me back to my girlhood, and they remind me of the days when I was younger, and I enjoy them, and I copy their mannerisms . . . and I love them.

On Mondays and Wednesdays they make me uncomfortable, because they represent a stage of behavior that I feel I've outgrown and that I wish the community as a whole would outgrow—on Mondays and Wednesdays.

And on Fridays and Sundays—on Fridays I'm completely apathetic—don't care one way or the other. And on Sundays I have a political commitment to their right to behave as they want.[32]

Marc's discomfort "on Mondays and Wednesdays" is quite common throughout the week in the gay subculture. It is this discomfort that creates the tension that relegates screaming queens to the fringes of the community. (Screamers *do* have entertainment value, though, which keeps them from being completely ostracized from the subculture. As Richard Kennedy says, *"In the bar* they're OK; they're cute; they're funny; they're like a sideshow attraction" [emphasis added; for "they're like a sideshow attraction" read "they're freaks"].)[33]

Some gays who adopt effeminate mannerisms continue to use them even after being acculturated. Those who remain flaming queens also often remain on the edges of the subculture. Their actions will, other gays fear, reinforce the stereotypes that gay activists have been trying to overcome for so long. Such men tend to identify themselves (although probably not consciously) as "they" rather than "we." This identification goes far beyond the idea that "we are the people our parents warned us about," a statement that still reflects the concept of "we." It is a "they" identity because it is a gay identity drawn from outside the gay world, an "exoteric we" identity.

This phenomenon is seen frequently among young gay men who have just come out. Many of them have no image of gays other than those depicted in stereotypes. Thus they begin to conform to the stereotypes, feeling that doing so is the best way to indicate that one is homosexual. Although such flaunting can represent a flouting of heterosexual values and may sometimes occur as a means of exploring feminine aspects of one's personality, this situation is different. The statement being made by these people is, "I am one of *them,*" rather than "I am one of *us.*" Thus these men have adopted an etic outsider's identification rather than an emic or insider's one in an attempt to accelerate the process of acculturation.[34]

Having been brought up in a heterosexual world, most gay people can effectively pass as straight: through years of socialization they have learned to function as members of the larger society. Within the gay subculture, the acculturation process occurs much more rapidly (relatively speaking), and appropriate patterns of behavior must be learned quickly. Although there is seldom direct conflict between any two of the many different groups to which a person may belong, gays find themselves in the position of belonging to two cultures that frequently exhibit contradicting values, mores, and behavior patterns. Gay people who fail to see beyond the stereotypes experience very strongly this cultural schizophrenia, which is the key to the exoteric we identity.

Conflict is not a prerequisite for acculturation except to the extent that it enhances subcultural cohesion. Rather, conflict and acculturation are related through the important role acculturation plays in dealing with stressful situations. When a person is at acculturation stages one and two (identification of self as gay and decision to associate with the subculture), he finds himself at odds with the culture in which he was raised. Coping with the resulting tensions and frustrations is difficult, making it very important that he reach level three (association with the subculture). Once level three has been attained, the gay community can provide the support needed in coping with conflict.

For the gay subculture, there is more than a grain of truth in the phrase "We have to laugh to keep from crying." The crying, however, is the result not of sadness, but of frustration; not of grief, but of anger. In *Nathan der Weise,* Lessing wrote, "Not all are free who mock their chains."[35] Homosexual people are far from free. They "mock their chains" and those that bind the straight culture as well. The struggle continues, as the folklore arising out of conflict situations illustrates. Verbal defiance of other groups may seem an inappropriate method of fighting the battle for liberation, but language is a powerful weapon when used effectively. Such defiance can point out the invalidity and harmfulness of stereotypes and prejudices. If insulting humor acts as a mirror in which people can see the senselessness of oppression and the pain it causes, much of the struggle will be over, allowing gays and straights to interact as people, not as types. As Alan Dundes has so accurately stated,

To the extent that folklore helps perpetuate racism, prejudice, male chauvinism, stereotypes, etc., we as professional folklorists must point this out at every opportunity. By making the unconscious or unselfconscious conscious, we may raise levels of consciousness. We cannot stop folklore, but we can hold it up to the light of reason and through the unrivaled picture it provides, we may better see what wrongs need righting.[36]

❦ 5

O Brave New World

AIDS, FOLKLORE, AND ACCULTURATION

IN STUDYING GAY ACCULTURATION we have to modify our concept of the acculturative process. Usually acculturation is seen as the movement of a minority or inferior group into membership in a larger, dominant group. The movement from a dominant culture to a subculture—in this case a stigmatized one—with culture and subculture sharing such features as ethnicities and nationality has not previously been studied from the point of view of acculturation. Gay acculturation is a sort of psychological immigration in which those making the transition retain valid passports that allow frequent return visits to their native culture. For these people the subculture (rather than the dominant group) becomes the significant other or group with which they identify, if not openly, then at least internally.

New members of the gay subculture tend to be quickly accepted. These newcomers identify with the significant group as they are accepted by it, a step essential for acculturation to continue. Still, they generally do not divest themselves of their straight cultural heritage. They are absorbed by the subculture, but they are not swallowed up and digested, because unlike many groups, the subculture itself is dependent on the straight world for much of its identity. This basic fact holds even if the identity is a reaction against some aspects of the straight culture: such a reaction is an attempt to define identity in terms of what the other group is not—for example, gay people are homosexual, straight people are not. Because of this peculiar relationship between gay and straight cultures, gay acculturation involves a degree of disassimilation from the straight world.

Gay acculturation is voluntary; it is sought rather than imposed, and membership in the dominant culture is almost always retained. Seeking membership in the subculture entails accepting the stigma associated with homosexuality, if only to fight the resulting oppression. Since no prestige and no economic benefits are associated with affiliation with the subculture, we must assume that the pressure of conflict and the need to be with like-minded others are stronger than the stigma and that sharing the stigma makes it less troublesome. Indeed, we have seen that gay folklore functions in these ways.

During acculturation one learns and internalizes folklore. One can manipulate a situation by choosing to foreground any of the contexts he perceives to be present; in this way he can relegate a previously primary context to a less important position and change the basis of the interaction.[1] When people are under stress, folklore comes into consciousness as a readily accessible—and generally acceptable—coping mechanism. Because of the opprobrium heaped upon the gay world, this use of folklore has become quite common in the subculture.

The gay community's unique position in relation to the straight world is also reflected in the ways the subculture uses its folklore. Although gays are marginal members of the dominant culture and can function at least as easily in the straight community as in the subculture, they nevertheless maintain a sense of territoriality.[2] Folklore is used to define territory by inhibiting outsiders' understanding of information; in this way nonmembers are excluded and the community is protected. Folklore aids in yet another aspect of territoriality—"mating" rituals—although in the case of the gay subculture, mating does not contribute to preservation of the species through offspring. Rather folklore functions like a mating ritual through maintenance, transmission, and validation of culture.

Folklore offers a framework for ordering experience; it also serves as a system for ordering reality. G. W. F. Hegel has pointed out that truth exists in two forms: *Wahrheit* (essential truth) and *Richtigkeit* (factual truth).[3] Although factual or objective truth is important, very few decisions are made based on facts. People's subjective views, their perceptions of truth, inform their actions, thereby affecting future objective truth. So too do gays' views of reality affect their actions, ultimately influencing the objective reality of the straight world.

This process sometimes requires disorganization and restructuring of our existing concept of reality. Part of this restructuring involves the elimination of formerly important cultural distinctions. Robert Darnton explains it this way:

[Squirrels] seem less threatening [than rats] because they belong unambiguously to the out-of-doors. It is the in-between animals, the neither fish-nor-fowl, that have special powers and therefore ritual values. . . . Hair, fingernail parings and feces . . . go into magic potions because they represent the ambiguous border areas of the body, where the organism spills over into the surrounding material world. All borders are dangerous. If left unguarded, they could break down, our categories collapse, and our world dissolve into chaos.[4]

Here in a nutshell we learn why the gay community is perceived by straights as posing such a great threat to the established social order. Gay people do not fit the comfortable categories of male and female; they do not conform to traditional sex roles. Many people are frightened by anything unfamiliar (especially when it is related to sexuality), and homosexuality has become an ideal target for the hostility arising from these fears.

Thus, by eliminating distinctions, gay people—especially through their folklore—are constantly restructuring reality, changing it in a sense. This process requires that the past be negated. Gay men in the subculture tend to see both the past and the future as the time they have spent and will spend in the straight world. The subculture rests on the threshold where that world of past and present is suspended—a willing suspension of belief. Yet, at the same time the subculture views itself hopefully as the future incorporate.

This last point can be better understood if we consider the gay world in terms of three cultural styles described by Margaret Mead in *Culture and Commitment:* the postfigurative, the cofigurative, and the prefigurative. In postfigurative cultures, change occurs very slowly; children learn to function in society from their elders, since the future will not be significantly different from the past. The elders retain control of society in cofigurative cultures, but young people model their behavior primarily on that of people of their own generation. Cofiguration tends to be a transitory stage for a culture passing temporarily out of and back into postfiguration or from postfiguration to prefiguration. Members of prefigurative cultures have experienced such rapid or drastic change that they have no models from whom to acquire cultural competence. Instead they must rely on their own skills and insights, and then become the models for their elders.[5]

Internally the gay subculture expresses all three styles: newcomers learning from older members, members learning from each other, and older members gaining increased understanding of homosexuality from newer members. In relation to the straight culture, however, the gay subculture is almost totally prefigurative. Since sexuality in the straight world is postfigurative—everyone is raised to be heterosexual (but bordering on asexual)—it is up to gays to teach straights ("the elders," in a sense) about sexuality in general and homosexuality in particular. Thus, in attempting to educate straight people about homosexuality as a part of its struggle for social change, the gay subculture is clearly prefigurative.

The gay community's response to the AIDS (acquired immunodeficiency syndrome) crisis is an excellent example of the prefigurative nature of the subculture. Even today the straight world is confused as to how to deal with AIDS; funding agencies—especially the United States government—are dragging their feet. But from the beginning of the crisis lesbians and gay men have mustered groups to educate the public, support people with AIDS, and fight for money for research and education. The straight community, unless it wants to reinvent the wheel, will have to take its cues from and learn from the gay world.

AIDS has brought new fears to the gay world. Not only do gay men fear disease and death; they also fear the rejection they face simply because AIDS is so closely associated in the public mind with homosexuality. The AIDS epidemic has caused some political setbacks for gay men and lesbians. It has made coming out more difficult than it has been for decades. In fact, it has chased many gay men back into the closet.

When AIDS was first publicized, many rumors circulated about the origins of the disease. Although we now know that AIDS is caused by a virus and is transmitted through exchange of body fluids, one of the early rumors was that it was the result of a clandestine germ warfare experiment carried out on gay men by the United States government. This rumor has been picked up by the Soviet media. Several reports in the Soviet Union, beginning in 1986, claim that AIDS leaked from a U.S. Army laboratory at Fort Detrick, Maryland.[6] The federal government has denied the charge.

More optimistic suggestions were that AIDS had implications for the origins of homosexuality. If Kaposi's sarcoma and pneumocystis carinii pneumonia (the two most common opportunistic infections associated with AIDS) struck only gay men, there must be an underlying genetic or hormonal cause of homosexuality. Such a discovery would discredit all the moral condemnations of homosexuality.

Eventually, people began to joke about AIDS, a typical response to stress. Almost all of the AIDS jokes that I have encountered are straight jokes. The following is one of the few gay AIDS jokes:

Do you know what the most difficult thing about having AIDS is?
Trying to convince your mother that you're part Haitian.

This joke expresses gay concerns; it says that death is less to be feared than is discovery of one's homosexuality. The majority of AIDS jokes convey messages of a much different sort:

Do you know why they haven't found a cure for AIDS yet?
They can't find two rats that will butt-fuck.

Based on the stereotype that gay men engage almost exclusively and obsessively in anal intercourse, which is assumed to be one of the primary modes of transmission of AIDS, this joke suggests that homosexuality is unnatural, that is, not occurring in nature.

AIDS was first diagnosed in 1981. At that time it was seen primarily as a gay problem; it received little media attention and there was little public awareness. Since early 1984, the situation has changed—AIDS is still seen as a gay disease, but media coverage has intensified and public awareness has increased greatly. A lot of AIDS jokes have been circulating, mainly in two waves tied to two events: the winter-spring 1984 media blitz focused the public's attention on AIDS, the disease was quickly dubbed "the gay plague," and a few jokes began to make the rounds; then, in the summer of 1985, actor Rock Hudson revealed that he had AIDS, and a renewed media push was quickly followed by a resurgence of the earlier AIDS jokes and the generation of many new ones, more than a few of which referred to Hudson himself.

AIDS is a great threat to gay men, less so to straight people, but even so the public rightly fears the disease. It could be seen as a castration complex—AIDS is in a sense both sexual and social castration, and death is the ultimate castration. Rarely is anything as nearly universally anxiety provoking as AIDS has proved to be. Nevertheless, the anxiety is greatest among gay men, and this difference is evident in the circulation of AIDS jokes. The jokes seem never to have been popular in the gay community, although they had a brief circulation.

The early AIDS jokes were few. In addition to the "buttfucking rats" joke were such queries as

Do you know what *gay* stands for?
Got AIDS yet?

What do you call a gay man in a wheelchair?
Roll-AIDS.

Among the many jokes about Rock Hudson are the following:

Do you know how AIDS got to California?
In an old Hudson.

Do you know what the difference between Rock Hudson and Ellis Island is?
Ellis Island is a ferry terminal.

Did you hear about the Rock Hudson Memorial Hospital?
It doesn't have any doctors or nurses, just aides.

Do you know what the biggest question in California is?
Who had the last piece of the Rock.

The jokes seem to fall into several categories. There are acronyms, such as the one for *gay* and the following:

Do you know what *AIDS* stands for?
Ass-Injected Death Sentence.
Already Infected Dick Sucker.
Another Infected Dick Sucker.
Adios, Infected Dick Sucker

There are puns, like the following:

Did you hear that the Centers for Disease Control in Atlanta have decided to set up an AIDS research center out at Stone Mountain?
They're going to call it "Sick Fags over Georgia."

(Six Flags over Georgia is a large amusement park outside Atlanta; Stone Mountain is a suburb of Atlanta named for the mountain-size granite boulder that is exposed there.)

In this category we also find the joke playing on Prudential Insurance Company's motto, "Get a Piece of the Rock," the one about AIDS getting to California in an old Hudson, and the Rock Hudson Memorial Hospital joke, as well as the following:

Did you hear that all the alligators in Florida are dying?
They have Gator-AIDS.

Did you hear about this deadly new disease that's going around?
It's called hearing-AIDS. You know how you get it? From listening to too many assholes.

Did you hear about the deadly disease going around in Carmel [an affluent suburb of Indianapolis]?
It's called MAIDS. You'll die if you don't have one.

There are racist AIDS jokes:

Do you know what sickle-cell anemia is?
AIDS for spades.

You know, they're going to have to change what they call AIDS.
All the blacks keep applying for it.

There are jokes that express the fear of contagion, like the Rock Hudson Memorial Hospital joke and the following:

Do you know how to give artificial respiration to an AIDS victim?
[Acted out: teller pretends to stomp on chest of someone lying on floor, blows toward face.]

Do you know how to keep from getting AIDS?
Sit on your ass and keep your mouth shut.

And there are moralizing jokes, including the previous one and this one:

Do you know what it says on Rock Hudson's tombstone?
Asses to ashes,
Lust to dust,
If you had tried pussy
You'd still be with us.

Both of these jokes deny the validity and the value of homosexual relationships.
So, why *do* people tell these jokes? They do not work as entertainment for the most part, but they do express attitudes and feelings. They are partly a reaction to the emphasis on AIDS in the media from time to time. They are also, and primarily, a reaction to homophobia and the fear of AIDS, which one person has labeled AfrAIDS.
Hudson's disclosure of his illness allowed AIDS to be used as a means for

people to express their feelings about gays. The jokes reinforce stereotypes and in doing so allow the tellers to make the psychologically comforting statement, "We won't be affected if we can keep them away from us and in their place." Thus, the jokes are a coping mechanism, but their effectiveness as such is limited; they relieve enough of the pressure, discomfort, and anxiety for people to avoid dealing with the real issue: AIDS is a lethal disease that attacks *people,* regardless of age, color, sex, sexual orientation, or any other variable; the virus does not discriminate. And even more, a major part of the issue that is being avoided is that gays are people just like everyone else.

Finally, the jokes provide a vehicle for bringing up a subject that is so serious and anxiety provoking that it might not be introduced into a conversation otherwise. I have several times heard conversations shift to AIDS after someone told an AIDS joke.

All of these functions are therapeutic.

As AIDS has continued to spread into the straight world, joking about AIDS has declined. For example, Liberace's death as a result of AIDS went almost unnoticed in the joke cycles. The few jokes now in circulation are of a different nature, as the following two examples show.

Did you hear about the two Polack junkies? They were shooting up one day, and one of them took the needle and shot up. And then the second one took the needle from the first one and shot up with it.

The first Polack said, "Are you crazy? Why did you shoot up with the same needle I used? Don't you know I have AIDS?"

And the second Polack said, "Oh, that's OK. I'm wearing a condom."

A little boy came home from school one day—he was about in the third grade. And he came home and his mother said, "Johnny, what did you learn in school today?"

Johnny said, "Well, we had sex education class."

His mother was kind of shook up, and she said, "Well, what did you learn about?"

And the little boy said, "We learned all about AIDS."

Well *that* really shook her up. So she said, "Well, what did you learn about AIDS?"

He said, "Well, you can't get it from a toilet seat, and you can't get it from kissing, and you really have to watch those intersections."

These jokes are fascinating because besides not being judgmental, they are educational. The first says, "If you're going to use intravenous drugs, don't share needles, and if you're going to have sexual relations, play safe." The second joke dispels mistaken ideas about transmission. It does contain a slight antigay, antidrug, antisex message in the apparent conflation of *homosexuals, injections,* and *intercourse* in the final word (a seeming play on the standard parental warning to "look both ways"). Nevertheless, it is primarily educational.[7]

The subject of AIDS has become more solemn, and the lore reflects this shift in tone. The following straight legend is from *USA Today*:

Wednesday night [22 October 1986], novelist Jackie Collins (*Hollywood Husbands*), ever the chronicler of sexual adventure, shared what she said was a true story on Joan Rivers' show.

A married Hollywood husband picked up a beautiful woman at a bar. They enjoyed a night of passion at a good hotel; in the morning he rolled over to find a sweet thank-you note. Class, he thought, real class. Then he walked into the bathroom and found, scrawled on the mirror in lipstick, "Welcome to the wonderful world of AIDS."

Not knowing if the woman had been kidding or not, he didn't dare have sexual relations with his wife, and it could be a long time before he'd know whether he had become an AIDS victim.[8]

This legend was widespread by early December 1986. In one version, the man went the next morning to be tested for AIDS and learned he did not have the disease. This variant makes it clear that people are still largely uneducated about AIDS: there is no test for AIDS per se, and it can take six months or more for the body to produce detectable antibodies to the virus.

Interestingly, the shift from gay-focused to straight-focused AIDS lore has resulted in the dropping of the moral and judgmental elements prevalent in the antigay AIDS jokes. There will probably be a few more AIDS legends, serving like the one above as cautionary tales. Then one will begin hearing personal experience narratives, first regarding acquaintances who have died, and then stories from people with AIDS themselves.

AIDS has become one more burden with which gay men must deal, one more source of stress making them turn to their subculture for support. Before getting that support, however, they must be acculturated and learn the traditions of the gay world.

By serving to validate gay life-styles, gay folklore affirms the integrity and worth of homosexual people. At the same time, it calls into question the standards imposed upon society by the straight culture, and in doing so frequently inverts and distorts these values. This invalidation of the rival group is especially pronounced in gay folklore because the subculture's norms conflict so strongly with those of straights. By twisting the mores of the straight culture, gay people in a very real sense invalidate the heterosexual world, saying not "gay is as good as," but "gay is better than."

Faced with insults, legal and physical threats, and other forms of abuse, gays have found that their folklore can also function to relieve tension, frustration, fear, and anxiety. By turning the tables on their oppressors, gays can achieve a psychological victory. By insulting other groups of people, gays can experience a feeling of superiority to *someone*, if not to everyone. It is extremely important for a person's emotional well-being that he not feel that he is inferior to everyone else.

The gay subculture developed as a result of the condemnation heaped upon it by the heterosexual world, generating in the process an extensive body of folklore. Until homosexuality is accepted as a natural manifestation of life, the various mechanisms at work in heterosexual enculturation cannot serve gay people adequately. Until homosexuality is viewed objectively and is discussed openly and without condemnation in our homes, schools, and other institutions, gay folklore will continue to be a major mechanism in acculturation within the gay subculture.

Afterword

THOUGH THIS BE MADNESS,
YET THERE IS METHOD IN IT

IN THIS STUDY I have limited my comments to the folklore of gay men. There are several reasons for excluding lesbian material from consideration. There is much less information available on lesbianism in general, thereby making the necessary background research much more difficult; I have few lesbian contacts, which would present problems in establishing a base for field work; and finally, the major obstacle is the separatist nature of a large part of the lesbian community in the city where I conducted most of my interviews. A female folklorist would much more likely be a successful collector and interpreter of lesbian folklore than would a male.[1]

I have placed an additional limitation upon my informants: my sample consists of openly homosexual men who actively participate in the gay subculture. In restricting my research base in this way, I may be accused of having skewed my data. My generalizations, therefore, should not be taken to be applicable to all homosexual people; neither should my conclusions be considered to apply in toto to any one person. Generalizations are merely compilations of the major attributes of the subject under study, representative of the type yet not actual examples of it. It would be a rare person indeed who exhibited all aspects of gay behavior discussed in this study. Gay folklore is a complex body of material held in trust by a large and only semivisible segment of our population.

I did most of my field work in Bloomington, Indiana, a city of about 50,000 with an additional population of 32,000 students enrolled at Indiana University. Bloomington is about fifty miles south of Indianapolis, and although it is a fairly small city, it has a disproportionately large, visible, and diverse gay community, at least in part because of the university. For this reason, the city serves as a sort of regional center for gay people from southern and central Indiana.[2]

A particular advantage of using Bloomington as my research base is the presence at Indiana University of the Alfred C. Kinsey Institute for Research in Sex, Gender, and Reproduction. The institute, among its other functions, houses the world's largest collection of materials related to sex research. Having access to that collection made my research much easier. Many of the manuscripts and rarer published items would have been almost impossible to find otherwise.

I observed and participated in the Bloomington gay community for seven years. I collected most of the material included in this study in Bloomington in 1981 and 1982. I have also had the opportunity of associating with gay people in nineteen other cities in nine midwestern and southern states and the District of Columbia.[3] These encounters took place in many gay bars, several gay restaurants, and at countless parties, picnics, and social gatherings.

Kenneth E. Read, in writing about a gay "tavern," points out a difference between the gay bar and other drinking establishments.

[The tavern] is a public place, and, unless you employ certain strategies that are learned only slowly, it is assumed that you may be approached and are familiar with the elements of the style. Your very presence means that you can't be ignorant.[4]

Although Read's comments are well founded, he fails to mention that normally in gay bars one must also use certain strategies if he wishes to be approached. Tactics both for being avoided and for being approached become even more important in "mixed" bars, where some of the men may be straight; the strategies come into play in attempting to discern a person's orientation, in trying to avoid rejection, and in seeking to avoid offending people.

Parties and other social events do not differ to any significant degree from those held and attended by nongay people, with again the possible exception of proxemics. Like the bar, however, and like their straight equivalents, these events do serve as active centers for transmitting folklore. As small groups break up and new ones form, as individuals float from one circle to another, items are passed on quickly;[5] jokes are especially susceptible to this form of rapid transmission, given the ease with which one learns a joke and the entertainment value associated with humor.[6]

Gay folklore is firmly tied to its context, so a textual analysis is insufficient for an understanding of the ways in which folklore functions within the subculture. Much of the meaning of the material comes from the situation and the performance. This study, therefore, is essentially analytic, based upon my observations; the interviews are supplemental. Given the types of situations in which the folklore is transmitted, it is very difficult to record in context, and subsequent interviews are mere shadows of the traditions as performed. Thus my recorded interviews serve to substantiate my observations and are a source of examples to accompany my analyses.

This study is written primarily from an "emic" point of view. An emic approach considers material from the insiders' point of view; an etic approach, on the other hand, relies upon the researcher's perceptions as an outsider.[7] Thus my emic approach may call my objectivity into question. Although no one can be completely objective, since it is impossible to divest oneself entirely of the myriad cultural attitudes through which all perceptions are filtered, analyzed, and judged, one can strive for objectivity. Such is my goal. Readers should bear in mind, however, that I am an insider, and my conclusions must be considered in the light of that fact. In addition, I have tried to take no stand on moral issues; I have attempted to refrain from making judgments—pro or con—concerning issues raised in my research. Rather, I have tried to report objectively what I have observed and to analyze this information as a folklorist, not as a moralist, not as a gay activist.

My desire for objectivity poses two problems. First, in presenting gay folklore to a larger, nongay audience, I am exposing details that help maintain the community and protect it from outsiders. Is such a revelation a violation of trust? I think not; much of the material I am dealing with has been written about before, although not from a folklorist's point of view. In addition, if this research helps develop a tolerance for the diversity among people, I think that something quite valuable will have been achieved. Second, it seems somewhat voyeuristic to include some of the personal experience narratives I have collected, particularly ones dealing with sexual encounters; to leave them out, on the other hand, would provide a less complete picture of gay folklore. And after all, those of us studying such topics are already voyeurs of a sort, as are our readers.

Finally, there are some very strong advantages that argue for an insider to do research of this type. Zora Neale Hurston has summarized these points in relation to the value of blacks collecting black folklore:

Folk-lore is not as easy to collect as it sounds. . . . [Blacks] are most reluctant at times to reveal that which their soul lives by. And the Negro, in spite of his open-faced laughter, his seeming acquiescence, is particularly evasive. You see we are a polite people and we do not say to our questioner, "Get out of here!" We smile and tell him or her something that satisfies the white person because, knowing so little about us, he doesn't know what he is missing. The Indian resists curiosity by a stony silence. The Negro offers a feather-bed resistance. That is, we let the probe enter, but it never comes out. It gets smothered under a lot of laughter and pleasantries.

The theory behind our tactics: "The white man is always trying to know into somebody else's business. All right, I'll set something outside the door of my mind for him to play with and handle. He can read my writing but he sho' can't read my mind. I'll put this play toy in his hand, and he will seize it and go away. Then I'll say my say and sing my song."[8]

The situation is similar for an outsider attempting to collect and analyze gay folklore. First of all, he or she must face the problem of making contact and developing rapport with a subculture that is still largely invisible; the collector must also establish a relationship of trust. Granted, these problems await most people undertaking field work, but they are compounded in dealing with gay folklore because of the stigmatization and isolation of gay people and the widespread reprobation directed toward them. In addition, being unfamiliar with the material, the researcher may have little idea what she or he is seeking; since most potential informants will not know what folklore is, they will be able to offer the collector little assistance. Thus formulating questions presents a great difficulty. If the folklorist succeeds in overcoming these obstacles, the problem still remains of the responses to his or her inquiries. If responses are forthcoming, they may seem flippant, even inverted, which can prove to be most frustrating.

This last point is particularly significant, in that it is closely related to the analysis of the material. A person unfamiliar with gay folklore may be unaware that humorous responses and inversion of standard values are typical within the subculture. Moreover, she or he may fail to realize that on occasion false answers may be given to create humor at the collector's expense. For this reason, the outsider runs the risk of obtaining invalid information unless he or she knows that giving false responses is itself a tradition of sorts and must be analyzed as such. An unfamiliarity with the culture almost guarantees a blindness to the richness of its traditions.[9]

Most of the works that have been published on gay folklore illustrate these shortcomings. Norine Dresser, in "'The Boys in the Band Is Not Another Musical': Male Homosexuals and Their Folklore," uses a Freudian framework to analyze jokes told by gay men. Although she does touch upon a few other traditions, she passes over them lightly; her narrow focus causes her to overlook much more than she sees. More significantly, her lack of understanding of gay culture results in her presentation of a very superficial analysis of her material. Dresser's limited involvement with gay people, detailed in her paper "'What's a Nice Girl like You Doing in a Place like This?': Problems of Doing Fieldwork in a Homosexual Bar," becomes quite apparent when one sees that she has altogether missed the major import of the jokes she collected. She sees the jokes functioning as a means of communication and providing a sense of membership, but she neglects internal conflicts (although she touches upon gay-straight oppositions), the inversion of heterosexual standards, the extensive use of and high value placed upon word play, and many other very important aspects of the gay tradition.[10]

Similar problems are evident in two works by Roy D. Smith. His "An Exploratory Consideration of Homosexual Folklore" deals with rumors that a number of well-known men and women have been homosexual.[11] His more-than-obvious conclusion is that these people serve as role models for gays. Not only did he fail to examine other aspects of gay folklore, he also neglected to explore the motivation underlying these rumors. He could have pointed out that some of the people purported to be gay serve as fantasy figures. He could have questioned the reasons certain people were mentioned much more often than others—persons like Tallulah Bankhead and Mae West, both of whom are extremely popular among gay men. Both women are nostalgia figures. It is frequently assumed that Bankhead was a lesbian because of her deep voice and strong, masculine personality; one of the traditions associated with Mae West asserts that she was actually a man in drag. The topic, then, of Smith's work was very rich, if narrow, and he failed to see any rationale for the rumors beyond the purely superficial level.

Smith's manuscript "Invert Folk Terminology" is a much more substantial study dealing with gay vocabulary and its acquisition and use. He slips up, though, when he makes the following statement:

Viewed from within homosexual society, [gay or "invert" language] would be slang; viewed from without it would be cant. Such a verbal distinction is without value, at least in the context of this study.[12]

Not only is a distinction between slang and cant valuable, it is an important aspect of the study of gay language. Among the many writers on this topic there has been little agreement upon the appropriate term, although I think that any linguist who has thoroughly studied the available information would agree that the gay language is actually an argot (or cant). It is definitely not slang, a faddish and transitory form of language. Discussion of the folk speech of the gay subculture can be carried out most clearly when it is seen and dealt with as an argot consisting of an extensive, relatively stable vocabulary, rules for use, and distinctive paralinguistic features.[13]

Esther Newton's *Mother Camp: Female Impersonation in America* gives a final example of the weaknesses that an outsider brings to a study of the gay male subculture.[14] Newton is an anthropologist, and her study of female impersonation is logically made from that point of view. On the whole, the book is well done, but Newton's analysis of two drag shows indicates the liabilities of limited esoteric knowledge.[15] A single illustration will suffice. The performer is telling a gay audience a version of "The Three Little Pigs" in which the third pig is gay. (See chapter 3 for the full text.)

> . . . **They all thought they'd build themselves some houses.** . . .
> **Sissy Pork** *(high voice)* **she built hers out of crepe paper and sequins** *(laughs),* **and she had a mirrored bedroom, much-used lace curtains** *(much laughter).* . . . **Why is it the girls always understand that and the boys never do? In other words, she done it up brown. Now we're back to the boys again. [Refers to anal intercourse: "the boys"—men who take the insertor *(sic)* role—do not understand.]**[16]

In her note Newton informs us that "done it up brown" "refers to anal intercourse." What she does not realize, and therefore cannot clarify for her readers, is that the humor here plays upon the earlier phrase "much-used lace curtains."

Lace curtains is a gay term for the foreskin; thus "much-used lace curtains" implies that Sissy Pork was quite promiscuous. This knowledge adds to the humor of the covert reference to anal intercourse. The narrator's audience obviously understood this implication. Newton also fails to point out that "the girls" are gay men, which explains why "the girls always understand that." It is odd that Newton would understand this use of *brown* and not catch the reference to lace curtains. According to Bruce Rodgers, use of *brown* in this way was dated when Newton did her research in the 1960s; *lace curtains*, on the other hand, was current in the argot, as it still is.[17]

I undertook this study to correct such problems. I hope that I have succeeded.

Informants

(All names are pseudonyms. Women's names are used for female impersonators. Most informants lived in Bloomington, Indiana, at the time of the interviews; those who lived elsewhere are so indicated. All interviews except those with Dorian Carr and Michelle Morgan and the second with Sabrina Focks were tape recorded. The tapes are in my possession.)

Rebecca Armstrong was born in Bedford, Indiana, in 1955. She is a high school graduate; she has worked as a female impersonator and as a waiter in Bloomington and Indianapolis. She has visited the Indianapolis gay community many times. Interviewed 1 April 1981.

Dorian Carr was born in Vincennes, Indiana, in 1946. He majored in accounting when in college and was working as a floral designer in Vincennes at the time of the interview. He has lived in Los Angeles and in Florida and has spent time in the gay communities of Indianapolis, Los Angeles, Atlanta, Cincinnati, Louisville, Chicago, Miami, Fort Lauderdale, and Tampa. Interviewed 8 November 1981.

Steve Daniels was born in Muncie, Indiana, in 1954. He was graduated from Ball State University with a bachelor of fine arts degree and now works for Ball State. He has spent time in the gay communities of New York, Chicago, Florida, Indianapolis, and Montreal. Interviewed 29 November 1982.

DeAnne Devereaux was born in 1958 in Indianapolis. She has completed some college work and is employed as a female impersonator. She has spent time in the gay community in Indianapolis. Interviewed 26 March 1981.

Christopher DuPont, born in Louisville in 1954, was a senior majoring in anthropology at Indiana University at the time of this interview. He has spent time in the gay communities of Indianapolis, Lafayette, and Louisville. He was interviewed with Marc Henderson, his roommate and lover, on 18 November 1981.

Thomas Evans was born in Bloomington in 1946. He earned his bachelor's and master's degrees in special education at Indiana University and has taught mentally handicapped students. Interviewed 18 November 1981.

Sabrina Focks was born in 1959 in Bloomington. She is a high school graduate and was working as a bouncer and bartender at the time of the interviews. She has been a female impersonator and still makes occasional guest appearances. She has also lived in Louisville and has spent time in the gay communities there and in Terre Haute, Indianapolis, and Columbus, Ohio. Interviewed 28 March 1981 and 18 November 1982.

Ramona Halston was born in 1959 in Tacoma, Washington, but grew up in Bedford, Indiana. At the time of the interview Ramona was studying to be a hairdresser and was working as a female impersonator. She holds the title of Miss Gay Ohio Valley, U.S.A. Interviewed 24 March 1981.

Marc Henderson was born in 1951 in Grand Rapids, Michigan. He has completed some graduate work and lists his profession as blue collar. Marc has lived in Paris and Chicago. He was interviewed with his roommate and lover, Christopher DuPont, on 18 November 1981.

John Herrick was born in Butte, Montana, in 1935. After earning bachelor's and master's degrees in English and a Ph.D. in American literature and French, he taught English for several years. He is now a realtor. He has lived in Ann Arbor, Denver, Rawlins (Wyoming), England, and France. He has visited gay communities in Ann Arbor, Detroit, Rawlins (Wyoming), San Francisco, Chicago, Indianapolis, New Orleans, Mexico City, Atlanta, New York, Key West, Montreal, Toronto, Quebec City, Paris, London, Rome, Florence, Poughkeepsie, Pittsburgh, Philadelphia, Taos (New Mexico), and Indiana (Pennsylvania). Interviewed 3 December 1981.

Richard Kennedy was born in Winchester, Indiana, in 1952. He was graduated from Indiana University with a degree in English education. At the time of the interview he was unemployed. He has lived in Illinois, West Virginia, New Jersey, New York, and California, but has associated with the gay community only in central Indiana. Interviewed 7 December 1981.

Darla Lee was born in Bedford, Indiana, in 1954. She is a high school graduate and works as a female impersonator and as a carpenter. She has visited the gay communities in Indianapolis, Louisville, and central Florida. Interviewed 2 May 1981.

Michael Monroe was born in Corning, New York, in 1953. He earned a B.A. in fine arts and comparative literature at Indiana University. At the time of the interview he was working as a recording engineer and a visual artist. He also lived in Columbus, Ohio, and Chicago, and spent time in the gay communities in those cities and in Houston. He died in 1985. Interviewed 1 December 1981.

Michelle Morgan was born in 1958 in Indianapolis. She has completed two years of college and works as a female impersonator. She lives in Indianapolis. Among other honors, she has been second runner-up in a Miss Gay Indiana pageant. She has spent time in the gay communities of Indianapolis, Anderson, Detroit, Cincinnati, and Columbus, Ohio. Interviewed 24 June 1981.

Hal Parmenter was born in 1935 in Indiana; he is a clergyman. He has also lived in New Haven (Connecticut), in London, in New York, and in Indianapolis, Seymour, and Rushville, Indiana. He has visited the gay communities in London, New York, New Haven, Boston, Toronto, Ottawa, York

(England), Edinburgh, Paris, Florence, Rome, Geneva, San Francisco, Los Angeles, Denver, St. Louis, Columbus (Ohio), Miami, New Orleans, Louisville, Indianapolis, Chicago, Detroit, and Des Moines. Interviewed 20 March 1981.

Bob Schultz was born in Nebraska in 1954. He has a master's degree in music from Indiana University. He has lived in Colorado and has spent time in the gay community in Topeka. Interviewed 3 December 1981.

Notes

INTRODUCTION

1. Sexual and obscene folklore have been almost totally avoided by folklorists. The major works that have been published include Frank A. Hoffman, *Analytical Study of Anglo-American Traditional Erotica* (Bowling Green, Ohio: Popular Press, 1973); Gershon Legman, *The Horn Book: Studies in Erotic Folklore* (New Hyde Park, N.Y.: University Books, Inc., 1964), *Rationale of the Dirty Joke: An Analysis of Sexual Humor,* first series (N.p.: Castle Books, 1968), *No Laughing Matter: Rationale of the Dirty Joke,* second series (New York: Bell Publishing Company, 1975), *The Limerick* (New York: Bell Publishing Company, 1964), and *The New Limerick: 2750 Unpublished Examples, American and British* (New York: Crown Publishers, 1977); and Vance Randolph, *Pissing in the Snow and Other Ozark Folktales* (Urbana: University of Illinois Press, 1976). See also Sandra K. D. Stahl, "Cursing and Its Euphemisms: Power, Irreverence, and the Unpardonable Sin," *Midwestern Journal of Language and Folklore* 3 (1977): 54–68, and *Journal of American Folklore* 75 (1962): 297, a special issue on folk literature and the obscene.

2. According to Kinsey, four percent of white males are exclusively homosexual throughout their lives; thirty-seven percent have at least some homosexual experience. The popular ten-percent figure is probably a combination of the figures for people classified as 5's and 6's on the Kinsey scale: a Kinsey 5 is predominantly homosexual; a 6 is exclusively same-sex oriented. See Alfred C. Kinsey, Wardell B. Pomeroy, and Clyde E. Martin, *Sexual Behavior in the Human Male* (Philadelphia: W. B. Saunders Company, 1948), pp. 623ff.

3. I explain the distinctions between *gay* and *homosexual* below.

4. John Boswell, *Christianity, Social Tolerance, and Homosexuality: Gay People in Western Europe from the Beginning of the Christian Era to the Fourteenth Century* (Chicago: University of Chicago Press, 1980), pp. 42–43; Panos D. Bardis, "A Glossary of Homosexuality," *Maledicta* 4 (1980): 59.

5. Boswell, *Christianity,* p. 43, n. 6; Bruce Rodgers, *Gay Talk: A [Sometimes Outrageous] Dictionary of Gay Slang* (New York: Paragon Books, 1979), p. 93.

6. Boswell, *Christianity,* pp. 42–43; Esther Newton, *Mother Camp: Female Impersonation in America* (Chicago: University of Chicago Press, 1972), p. 22; Greer Trotter Warren, "Silence Keeping: Conversations with Two Lesbians" (unpublished manuscript in the author's possession), p. 24; George Weinberg, *Society and the Healthy Homosexual* (New York: St. Martin's Press, 1972), pp. 69–70; David Lee Cornelius, "An Application of Rules-Based Theory of Interpersonal Communication: The Rules of Taboo Communication within a 'Gay Community'" (Ph.D. diss., Florida State University, 1980), p. 136; Charles Stone, "The Semantics of Gay," *The Advocate,* 3 September 1981, 20–22.

Apparently unaware of the long history of the word *gay,* in 1980 John Ciardi wrote, "[*Queer* has] most recently [been] replaced by *gay,* but speaking for the Society of Overaged Heterosexuals Who Would Yet Enjoy Gaiety, and with no particular malice toward homosexuals, I insist on resenting this usurpation of a word to which I once had a full and fair right" (*A Browser's Dictionary and Native Guide to the Unknown American Language* [New York: Harper & Row, Publishers, 1980], p. 324). Ciardi fails to realize that although *gay* "homosexual" and *gay* "joyous" happen to be homophonous, they are in all probability two different words with distinct etymologies. In 1983 he softened his tone somewhat, writing, "Homosexual activists seized on [*gay*] because they needed it as the most acceptable term for 'social merchandising.' I need it too, and can no longer use it as I would wish to, but their need is prob. greater; let them have it and may we all be merry, if not gay." [All *sic.*] (*A Second Browser's Dictionary and Native Guide to the Unknown American Language* [New York: Harper & Row, Publishers, 1983], p. 113.)

7. Cornelius, "Rules-Based Theory," p. 136.

8. Grace Sims Holt, " 'Inversion' in Black Communication," in *Rappin' and Stylin' Out: Communication in Urban Black America,* ed. Thomas Kochman (Urbana: University of Illinois Press, 1972), p. 154.

9. Holt, "Inversion," p. 156.

10. Kenneth Plummer, *Sexual Stigma: An Interactionist Account* (London: Routledge & Kegan Paul, 1975), pp. 98–100.

11. Kenneth E. Read (*Other Voices: The Style of a Male Homosexual Tavern* [Novato, Calif.: Chandler & Sharp, Publishers, Inc., 1980]) has used Jean Genet's image of a hall of mirrors in discussing gay values and "styles" (the term he uses since he denies the presence of a gay subculture). Laud Humphreys and Brian Miller ("Identities in the Emerging Gay Culture," in *Homosexual Behavior: A Modern Reappraisal,* ed. Judd Marmor [New York: Basic Books, Inc., 1980]) refer to these distortions as refractions (pp. 146–47).

1. Coming to Terms

1. Barbara Weightman, "Gay Bars as Private Places," *Landscape* 24 (1980): p. 10.

2. Meredith R. Ponte, "Life in a Parking Lot: An Ethnography of a Homosexual Drive-In," in *Deviance: Field Studies and Self-Disclosures,* ed. Jerry Jacobs (Palo Alto, Calif.: National Press Books, 1974), p. 7.

3. John Boswell, *Christianity, Social Tolerance, and Homosexuality: Gay People in Western Europe from the Beginning of the Christian Era to the Fourteenth Century* (Chicago: University of Chicago Press, 1980), p. 59.

4. Ibid.

5. Vito Russo, *The Celluloid Closet: Homosexuality in the Movies* (New York: Harper & Row, Publishers, 1981), p. 6.

6. Ruth Benedict, *Patterns of Culture* (Boston: Houghton Mifflin Company, 1934), pp. 7–8.

7. Carol A. B. Warren, *Identity and Community in the Gay World* (New York: John Wiley & Sons, 1974), pp. 5, 98.

8. Maurice Leznoff and William A. Westley, "The Homosexual Community," *Social Problems* 3 (1956): 257.

9. William M. Hoffman, ed., *Gay Plays: The First Collection* (New York: Avon Books, 1979), p. xxxv.

10. Boswell, *Christianity,* pp. 333–34.

11. Salvatore John Licata, "Gay Power: A History of the American Gay Movement, 1908–1974" (Ph.D. diss., University of Southern California, 1978); Toby Marotta, *The Politics of Homosexuality* (Boston: Houghton Mifflin Company, 1981); "4 Policemen Hurt in 'Village' Raid," *New York Times,* 30 June 1969, p. 22, col. 1.

12. Edmund White, *States of Desire: Travels in Gay America* (New York: E. P. Dutton; paperback edition: Bantam Books, 1981), p. 105.

13. Licata, "Gay Power," pp. 230–31.

14. For example, see Howard Brown, *Familiar Faces, Hidden Lives: The Story of Homosexual Men in America* (New York: Harcourt, Brace, Jovanovich, 1976), p. 43.

15. C. W. von Sydow, "On the Spread of Tradition," in *Selected Papers on Folklore,* ed. Laurits Bødker (Copenhagen: Rosenkilde and Bagger, 1948).

16. Barre Toelken, *The Dynamics of Folklore* (Boston: Houghton Mifflin Company, 1979), p. 51.

17. Dan Ben-Amos, "Toward a Definition of Folklore in Context," in *Toward New Perspectives in Folklore,* ed. Américo Paredes and Richard Bauman (Austin: University of Texas Press, 1972), pp. 12–13.

18. Dell Hymes, *Foundations in Sociolinguistics* (Philadelphia: University of Pennsylvania Press, 1974), p. 5.

19. James P. Spradley and Brenda J. Mann, *The Cocktail Waitress: Woman's Work in a Man's World* (New York: John Wiley & Sons, 1975), p. 6; Kenneth E. Read, *Other Voices: The Style of a Male Homosexual Tavern* (Novato, Calif.: Chandler & Sharp Publishers, Inc., 1980), pp. 176–78.

20. Kenneth Plummer, *Sexual Stigma: An Interactionist Account* (London: Routledge & Kegan Paul, 1975), p. 159.

21. Erving Goffman, *Frame Analysis: An Essay on the Organization of Experience* (New York: Harper & Row, Publishers, 1974), p. 10.

22. Alf H. Walle, "Getting Picked Up without Being Put Down: Jokes and the Bar Rush," *Journal of the Folklore Institute* 13 (1976): 203.

23. Sally Yerkovich, "Conversational Genres," in *Handbook of American Folklore,* ed. Richard M. Dorson (Bloomington: Indiana University Press, 1983), p. 278.

24. Toelken, *Dynamics,* p. 12.

25. Walle, "Getting Picked Up without Being Put Down," 213–14.

26. Ibid., 212.

27. Plummer, *Sexual Stigma,* p. 193.

28. Yerkovich, "Conversational Genres," p. 279.

29. Walle, "Getting Picked Up without Being Put Down," 206, 213–14.

2. It Takes One to Know One

1. See Henry Hiż, "Logical Basis of Semiotics"; Thomas A. Sebeok, "Ecumenicalism in Semiotics"; and Rulon S. Wells, "Criteria for Semiosis," all in *A Perfusion of Signs,* ed. Thomas A. Sebeok (Bloomington: Indiana University Press, 1977).

2. Edmund White, *States of Desire: Travels in Gay America* (New York: E. P. Dutton, 1980), p. 248. See also Edward William Delph, *The Silent Community: Public Homosexual Encounters* (Beverly Hills: Sage Publications, 1978), p. 115, and Barbara Weightman, "Gay Bars as Private Places," *Landscape* 24 (1980), passim.

3. Sherri Cavan, *Liquor License: An Ethnography of Bar Behavior* (Chicago: Aldine Publishing Company, 1966), p. 190.

4. Other gay subcultures have also developed distinctive argots. John Boswell, in *Christianity, Social Tolerance, and Homosexuality: Gay People in Western Europe from the Beginning of the Christian Era to the Fourteenth Century* (Chicago: University of Chicago Press, 1980), states that the European gay subculture of the High Middle Ages "appears to have had its own slang" (p. 253). In contemporary Greece gays speak a language of their own as well. It parallels gay English in many ways, having special meanings for words and using paralinguistic features similar to those used by American gays. As Steve A. Demakopoulos states in "The Greek Gays Have a Word for It" (*Maledicta* 2 [1978]),

Though much of the unintelligibility of *Kaliarda* is certainly due to its esoteric vocabulary, perhaps as much can be ascribed to a very particular diction and pronunciation, as well as to an extraordinary speed of delivery. This, when accompanied by expressive gestures, mincing grimaces and feminine body movements, results in an inimitable mimicry of sound and sight.(33)

5. Evelyn Hooker, "The Homosexual Community," in *Proceedings of the XIV International Congress of Applied Psychology* (Copenhagen: Munksgaard, 1961), p. 144; Kenneth E. Read, *Other Voices: The Style of a Male Homosexual Tavern* (Novato, Calif.: Chandler & Sharp Publishers, Inc., 1980), p. 35; and White, *States of Desire,* p. 194.

6. I discuss camp in chapter 3, which deals with cohesion.

7. Esther Newton, *Mother Camp: Female Impersonation in America* (Chicago: University of Chicago Press, 1972), p. 56, and Julia P. Stanley, "Homosexual Slang," *American Speech* 45 (1970): 55, touch on the significance of verbal agility among gay men.

8. John Reid, *The Best Little Boy in the World* (New York: Ballantine Books, 1973 [revised edition: 1976]), p. 192.

9. Alf H. Walle ("Getting Picked Up without Being Put Down: Jokes and the Bar Rush," *Journal of the Folklore Institute* 13 [1976]) discusses the use of humor in changing the level of intimacy of a conversation.

10. Grace Sims Holt, " 'Inversion' in Black Communication," in *Rappin' and Stylin' Out: Communication in Urban Black America,* ed. Thomas Kochman (Urbana: University of Illinois Press, 1972), pp. 153, 154.

11. David W. Maurer, "The Argot of Narcotic Addicts," in *Readings in American Dialectology,* ed. Harold B. Allen and Gary N. Underwood (New York: Appleton-Century-Crofts, 1971), p. 503.

12. Bruce Rodgers, *Gay Talk: A (Sometimes Outrageous) Dictionary of Gay Slang* (New York: Paragon Books, 1979), p. 14; Stanley, "Homosexual Slang," 5.

13. This fact holds, despite Stanley's contention in "Gay Slang/Gay Culture: How Are They Related?" (paper read at the 1974 annual meeting of the American Anthropological Association, in the collection of the Alfred C. Kinsey Institute for Research in Sex, Gender, and Reproduction, Indiana University Bloomington) that "only *camp* and *closet* and their related groups of words can be said to be uniquely gay in that these sets of words have not been borrowed from other groups" (p. 8). Joseph J. Hayes repeats part of Stanley's comment verbatim (without quotation marks) in "Lesbians, Gay Men, and Their 'Languages' " (in *Gayspeak,* ed. James W. Chesebro [New York: The Pilgrim Press, 1981], p. 39).

14. Hooker, "The Homosexual Community," pp. 52, 53.

15. Paul H. Gebhard, "Homosexual Socialization," *Excerpta Medica International Congress Series No. 150* (Madrid: Proceedings of the IV World Congress of Psychiatry, 1966), p. 1029. Stanley, in "Homosexual Slang," says the rapid dissemination is a result of "the transient nature of the homosexual subculture" (46). Gays, however, seem to be no more transient than other Americans.

16. Graffiti presents an awkward problem in distinguishing between verbal and nonverbal folklore: it is verbal, and yet it is not oral. I have chosen not to deal with graffiti in any detail, because most graffiti, while homoerotic in content, is apparently written by (supposedly) straight men. There tends to be very little graffiti in the restrooms of gay establishments. Gershon Legman, however, feels that "modern inscriptions . . . [are] mostly homosexual in . . . *intent*" ("Homosexuality and Toilet Inscriptions—An Analysis," unpublished manuscript, 1940–41, in the collection of the Alfred C. Kinsey Institute for Research in Sex, Gender, and Reproduction, Indiana University Bloomington, p. T.2; emphasis added). He concludes his analysis of graffiti with the following statement:

It is perhaps worth noting that almost invariably the pictograph [accompanying an illustrated graffito] is above the inscription, signifying usually that it was drawn first—drawn, one might add, right out of the twisted, tortured mind of the frustrated and abnormal sort of creature who scratches furtive homosexual inscriptions on toilet walls. (p. T.5)

More than enough said.

17. White, *States of Desire,* p. 92.

18. John Ciardi, *A Browser's Dictionary and Native Guide to the Unknown American Language* (New York: Harper & Row, Publishers, 1980), p. 323.

19. White, *States of Desire,* p. 42. Castro Street is in the gay district in San Francisco.

20. Walle, "Getting Picked Up without Being Put Down," 201. See also Erving Goffman, *Behavior in Public Places* (London: Collier-MacMillan Ltd., The Free Press of Glencoe, 1963), pp. 245–46.

21. William H. Martineau, "A Model of the Social Functions of Humor," in *The Psychology of Humor,* ed. Jeffrey H. Goldstein and Paul H. McGhee (New York: Academic Press, 1972), p. 103.

22. Interview with John Herrick, 3 December 1981.

23. Jacob Levine, "Regression in Primitive Clowning," in *Motivation in Humor,* ed. Jacob Levine (New York: Atherton Press, 1969); Isaac Asimov, "Humor," in *Opus 200,* ed. Isaac Asimov (Boston: Houghton Mifflin Company, 1979), p. 240.

24. Rodgers *(Gay Talk)* offers the following variant:

Two gay boys were browsing in a bookstore; suddenly one turned to the other asking, "Do you prefer Kipling to Browning?" to which the other blushingly replied, "I don't know—how do you kiple?" (p. 121)

25. "Reach out and touch someone" is an advertising slogan of the American Telephone and Telegraph Company.

26. Interview with Michael Monroe, 1 December 1981.

27. Interview with Dorian Carr, 8 November 1981.

28. Interview with John Herrick, 3 December 1981.

29. Hayes, "Lesbians, Gay Men, and Their 'Languages,'" p. 37. See also Laud Humphreys, *Out of the Closets: The Sociology of Homosexual Liberation* (Englewood Cliffs, N.J.: Prentice-Hall, Inc., 1972), p. 67.

30. See Hal Fischer, *Gay Semiotics ♂: A Photographic Study of Visual Coding among Homosexual Men* (San Francisco: NSF Press, 1977), passim; Hayes, "Lesbians, Gay Men, and Their 'Languages,'" pp. 37 and 42; and Edward Sagarin, "Language of the Homosexual Subculture," *Medical Aspects of Human Sexuality* 4 (1970): 40.

31. "The History of the Lambda," *Gaylife,* 27 March 1981, p. 23. See also Toby Marotta, *The Politics of Homosexuality* (Boston: Houghton Mifflin Company, 1981), p. 145n.

32. Heinz Heger, *The Men with the Pink Triangle,* trans. David Fernbach (Boston: Alyson Publications, Inc., 1980), passim.

33. Interview with Hal Parmenter; see also Lynn Ramsey, *Gigolos: The World's Best Kept Men* (Englewood Cliffs, N.J.: Prentice-Hall, Inc., 1978), p. 119. Although his work is not completely dependable, see Fischer *(Gay Semiotics)* for more information on gay nonverbal communication.

34. According to Havelock Ellis, during the early twentieth century red neckties indicated a homosexual orientation (quoted in Jonathan Katz, *Gay American History: Lesbians and Gay Men in the U.S.A.* [New York: Avon, 1976], p. 81). Fischer *(Gay Semiotics)* claims that the use of bandanas grew out of the leather culture (p. 20); Hayes ("Lesbians, Gay Men, and Their 'Languages'") suggests a more curious origin: "This custom seems to have originated in nineteenth-century Colorado mining towns, where men with pocket bandanas played 'follower' and those without played 'leader' at Friday night dances where there were few or no women present" (p. 36).

35. Read, *Other Voices,* p. 12.

36. For more about eye contact and its implications—as well as about cruising—

among both gays and straights, see Cavan, *Liquor License,* p. 190; Delph, *The Silent Community,* pp. 50–51 and 121; Norine Dresser, "'The Boys in the Band Is Not Another Musical': Male Homosexuals and Their Folklore," *Western Folklore* 33 (1974): 208–209; Desmond Morris, *Manwatching: A Field Guide to Human Behavior* (New York: Harry N. Abrams, Inc., 1977) pp. 71–72, 77, and 246; and James P. Spradley and Brenda J. Mann, *The Cocktail Waitress: Woman's Work in a Man's World* (New York: John Wiley & Sons, Inc., 1975), pp. 102 and 107.

37. Morris, *Manwatching,* pp. 130–31.

38. David Sonenschein, "The Homosexual's Language," *Sex Research* 5 (1969): 290. See also Donald Webster Cory, "The Language of the Homosexual," *Sexology* 32 (1965): 163; Maurer, "Argot of Addicts," p. 504; and Sagarin, "Language of the Homosexual Subculture," 39.

3. THERE'S NO VERSION LIKE PERVERSION

1. Sigmund Freud, *Jokes and Their Relation to the Unconscious,* trans. James Strachey (New York: W. W. Norton & Co., Inc., 1960), p. 10.

2. It is interesting to compare this joke with the following one quoted by Norine Dresser:

Did you hear about the two gay boys that were living together?
One of 'em got the mumps and the other started knitting little things.

("'The Boys in the Band Is Not Another Musical': Male Homosexuals and Their Folklore," *Western Folklore* 33 [1974]: 211.)

3. Carol Mitchell, in "A Comparison of Heterosexual Feminist and Lesbian Feminist Jokes" (paper presented at the 1981 annual meeting of the American Folklore Society, in the author's possession), gives the following variant:

Two elephants are standing on a street corner and they see this naked man run by. One turns to the other and says, "How do you suppose he can breathe through that little thing?" (p. 4)

4. The joke is a pun on the name of a brand of liniment.

5. The first line is quoted in Bob Milne, "Defiant and Deviant!" *Sexual Behavior* (March 1973): 28.

6. Dresser, "'The Boys in the Band,'" 211.

7. Esther Newton, *Mother Camp: Female Impersonation in America* (Chicago: University of Chicago Press, 1972), pp. 76–77. A roach is the butt of a marijuana cigarette; "I don't go that route" means "I'm straight."

8. A. R. Radcliffe-Brown, *Structure and Function in Primitive Society* (New York: The Free Press, 1965), pp. 90–91, as quoted in James P. Spradley and Brenda J. Mann, *The Cocktail Waitress: Woman's Work in a Man's World* (New York: John Wiley & Sons, Inc., 1975), p. 89.

9. Dresser, "'The Boys in the Band,'" 211–12.

10. Interview with Bob Schultz, 3 December 1981.

11. David Sonenschein, "Homosexual Humor," *Sexual Behavior* 3 (March 1973): 30.

12. Dresser, "'The Boys in the Band,'" 210.

13. Ibid., 209.

14. The narrator was trying to suggest his homosexuality to two other gay men in the audience; he had been told of their sexual orientation before he met them.

15. Compare with the following version from Newton, *Mother Camp* (pp. 74–75):

Everybody knows George and Tony. And they were out havin' a . . . Chesterfield you know, suckin' up a beer? Well it was before the show. And all of a sudden, this man walked in, wearin' one of them . . . he's wearing one of these suits, I know you've seen them. They're all striped, chartreuse, pink, and lavender? He said, "Hey George, I'll make you a five-buck bet that one's gonna order a pink lady." The man said (*in a loud masculine voice*), "I'll have a straight shot with water back." He said, "O.K., lost the first five bucks, still bet she's gonna order a pink lady." The man said, "I know what the hell you're talkin' about. You're talkin' about my suit." He said, "It ain't my fault. I sent my wife out to buy it. I told her, I said, 'Honey, would you go out to Cox's and buy a seersucker suit?' and she went to Sears."

16. "Get Up and Bar the Door" is a ballad in which a husband and wife have an agreement that the first one to speak will have to bar the door, since neither one wants to get up and do it. Two men enter the house, eat the food, and are about to cut off the man's beard and kiss the woman when the man protests. At that point the woman tells him that since he has spoken first, he must get up and bar the door.

17. Evelyn Hooker, "The Homosexual Community," in *Proceedings of the XIV International Congress of Applied Psychology* (Copenhagen: Munksgaard, 1961), p. 56; Julia P. Stanley, "Homosexual Slang," *American Speech* 45 (1970): 54; C. A. Tripp, *The Homosexual Matrix* (New York: Signet, 1976), pp. 173–78.

18. Susan Sontag, "Notes on 'Camp,'" *Partisan Review* 31 (1964): 519; Alan Brien, "Camper's Guide," *New Statesman* 23 June 1967, 873; interview with Michael Monroe, 1 December 1981; Leonard R. N. Ashley, "'Lovely, Blooming, Fresh and Gay': The Onomastics of Camp," *Maledicta* 4 (1980): 228.

19. Sontag, "Notes," 529.

20. "A Vest-Pocket Guide to CAMP," *Life,* 20 August 1965, p. 84.

21. Newton, *Mother Camp,* p. 107.

22. Michael Bronski, *Culture Clash: The Making of Gay Sensibility* (Boston: South End Press, 1984), p. 42.

23. Edmund White, *States of Desire: Travels in Gay America* (New York: E. P. Dutton, 1980), pp. 235–36; emphasis in last phrase added.

24. Tripp, *The Homosexual Matrix,* p. 269; Brien, "Camper's Guide," 874.

25. Newton, *Mother Camp,* p. 105; Sontag, "Notes," 529; "Vest-Pocket Guide," p. 84.

26. Vito Russo, "Camp," in *Gay Men: The Sociology of Male Homosexuality,* ed. Martin P. Levine (New York: Harper & Row, Publishers, 1979), p. 210.

27. Interviews with Marc Henderson (18 November 1981), John Herrick (3 December 1981), and Michael Monroe (1 December 1981).

28. Interview with Hal Parmenter, 20 March 1981. Compare with the following variant from Milne, "Defiant and Deviant!" (p. 28):

A classic in-joke of the 40s was the one about a famous Catholic cardinal familiarly known by a feminine name who, since homosexuality transcends all boundaries, invited a fellow clergyman from a Protestant denomination to attend a high mass in which he officiated. The minister was much impressed by the theatricality and panoply of the cathedral and the service. As the prelate swept down the aisle in full regalia, lace overshirt, red velvet and ermine cape, silk hat, etc., swinging the smoking censer, the minister leaned out from his pew and whispered, "I love your drag, but pssst—your purse is on fire."

Also compare with this version from Ashley, "Onomastics of Camp" (236):

Who will now tell some modern equivalent of "Bubbles," Cardinal Spellman: "I love your fab[ulous] drag, honey, but [eying the swinging censer] your purse is on fire"? [All *sic*.]

29. Ashley, "Onomastics of Camp," 237.

30. Another version uses "director" instead of "young man." A third version is the following:

My *favorite* one is the one about when somebody came up to Tallulah—except I heard it about [another actress] . . . and said, "Darling, do you realize that your hairdresser's gay?" And she said, "Well, he hasn't ever sucked *my* cock."
. . . I like that one, because it gives the gays a good—shows the good side.

31. For example, see Sandra K. D. Stahl, "Personal Experience Stories," in *Handbook of American Folklore,* ed. Richard M. Dorson (Bloomington: Indiana University Press, 1983), p. 270, and James P. Leary, "White Guys' Stories of the Night Street," *Journal of the Folklore Institute* 14 (1977): 66.

32. Stahl, "Personal Experience Stories," p. 274.

33. White, *States of Desire,* p. 101.

34. Interview with Steve Daniels, 29 November 1982.

35. Interview with John Herrick, 3 December 1981.

36. Interview with Hal Parmenter, 20 March 1981. This version of Hal's narrative is somewhat stilted. I have heard him tell the story on quite a few occasions, always more relaxed than the rendition quoted here. He attributed his tense manner to being "used to dictating" when confronted with a tape recorder.

37. Interview with Ramona Halston, 24 March 1981. The narrator is a female impersonator. Punk rock is a style of music made popular in the early 1980s. Fans of punk music wear bizarre costumes and makeup; for example, they often have close-cropped hair; dye their hair green, purple, orange, and other colors; and use safety pins as earrings and other forms of jewelry.

38. Interview with Hal Parmenter, 20 March 1981.

39. Interview with Ramona Halston, 24 March 1981.

40. Interview with Hal Parmenter, 20 March 1981. The third and fourth paragraphs of this excerpt were elicited by a follow-up question and were inserted out of order. This section was an integral part of this story the times I had heard Hal tell it; for some reason he initially left it out of this rendition.

41. Newton, *Mother Camp,* p. 10.

42. Both ibid.

43. Ibid., p. 5, n. 14.

44. Roger Baker, *Drag: A History of Female Impersonation on the Stage* (London: Triton Books, 1968), pp. 52–53.

45. Ibid., p. 25.

46. Quoted in Jonathan Katz, *Gay American History: Lesbians and Gay Men in the U.S.A.* (New York: Avon, 1976), p. 72; see also pp. 66 and 68.

47. Beverly Stoeltje, "Festival in America," in *Handbook of American Folklore,* ed. Richard M. Dorson (Bloomington: Indiana University Press, 1983), pp. 240, 243.

48. Interview with Rebecca Armstrong, 1 April 1981; the mother-daughter relationship was also discussed by Michelle Morgan (24 June 1981), Ramona Halston (24 March 1981), and DeAnne Devereaux (26 March 1981).

49. Barbara Kirshenblatt-Gimblett, "Studying Immigrant and Ethnic Folklore," in *Handbook of American Folklore,* ed. Richard M. Dorson (Bloomington: Indiana University Press, 1983), p. 40.

50. Interview with Darla Lee, 2 May 1981. The Omni was a gay bar in Bloomington during the late 1970s.

51. Ibid.

52. Interview with Rebecca Armstrong, 1 April 1981.

53. Ibid.

54. Interview with Sabrina Focks, 18 November 1982.
55. Interview with Ramona Halston, 24 March 1981.
56. Newton, *Mother Camp,* p. 46.
57. Interview with Rebecca Armstrong, 1 April 1981.
58. White, *States of Desire,* p. 179; interview with John Herrick, 3 December 1981.
59. Maurice Leznoff and William A. Westley, "The Homosexual Community," *Social Problems* 3 (1956): 258.

4. Better Blatant than Latent

1. For a good survey of the legal problems homosexual people face see John Rechy, *The Sexual Outlaw* (New York: Dell Publishing Co., Inc., 1977).
2. William H. Martineau, "A Model of the Social Functions of Humor," in *The Psychology of Humor,* ed. Jeffrey H. Goldstein and Paul H. McGhee (New York: Academic Press, 1972), p. 118.
3. Kenneth E. Read, *Other Voices: The Style of a Male Homosexual Tavern* (Novato, Calif.: Chandler & Sharp Publishers, Inc., 1980), p. xvii.
4. Validation of culture is one of the four functions of folklore identified by William R. Bascom. The other functions he defines are education, ensuring conformity to cultural norms, and offering a psychological means of escaping repression. See "Four Functions of Folklore," in *The Study of Folklore,* ed. Alan Dundes (Englewood Cliffs, N.J.: Prentice-Hall, Inc., 1965), pp. 279–98. İlhan Başgöz adds a fifth function to Bascom's list: social protest ("Protest: The Fifth Function of Folklore," manuscript, 1982, in author's possession).
5. Read, *Other Voices,* p. 17.
6. Walter Lippmann, *Public Opinion* (New York: The Free Press, 1922), p. 6.
7. Ibid., pp. 78, 81–82.
8. Ibid., p. 82.
9. John Boswell, *Christianity, Social Tolerance, and Homosexuality: Gay People in Western Europe from the Beginning of the Christian Era to the Fourteenth Century* (Chicago: University of Chicago Press, 1980), p. 273.
10. Interview with Hal Parmenter, 20 March 1981. The legend has been used as the basis of a mystery novel by Tony Fennelly, *The Glory Hole Murders* (New York: Carroll & Graf Publishers, Inc., 1985). I have heard variants of this legend from all over the United States. Fragmented versions were reported by Marc Henderson and Christopher DuPont (18 November 1981) and by Michael Monroe (1 December 1981):

Joe: There's one in particular I have in mind involving a glory hole.
Christopher: Yes?
Joe: Do you know the story?
Christopher: I don't know; go on.
Joe: Well, I don't want to tell it; I want *you* to tell it if you know it.
Christopher: Involving a glory hole?
Joe: Yes. Someone who goes in and the person on the other side . . .
Marc: Armed and extremely dangerous?
Christopher: . . . And sticks a straight pin through the cock?
Marc: Oh, I've heard that story.
Joe: Yes, tell me the story the way you've heard it.
Christopher: Oh, I just hear that there's somebody who nobody's been able to point out to me that goes in there and gets down on their knees and looks through and sticks their finger through, and when you stick your cock through they stick a straight pin through your cock. . . .
Joe: Where did this take place?
Christopher: Well, it wasn't going around in '75, I'll tell you that. . . .

Joe: Where'd you hear about it?

Christopher: In the last year at the bookstore.

Marc: I was never told of it as a tale, something that had actually happened. I have read that incident in a porno novel, and I've heard it mentioned as a comic suggestion for revenge against someone.

Michael: The only legend I know is where you stick your dick through and somebody puts a hatpin through it so you can't pull it out.

Joe: Have you ever heard that told as something that really happened?

Michael: Only in the sense that it was a friend of a friend of a friend, and by that time I consider it a legend.

Joe: Yes. Where was it supposed to have taken place?

Michael: I was told it in Chicago. I don't remember if it was given a locale.

Another informant told me the following version, which he had heard "told as true" in Iowa City in 1952 or 1953:

> There was a drugstore in Iowa City with stairs inside to a bathroom in the basement that people would come in off the street to use. There were two stalls or a stall and a urinal with a glory hole. Gays would meet there, and the police would harass them. One day an undercover cop went in there, and this gay man recognized him. He'd been lying in wait for him, so when the undercover policeman stuck his penis through the glory hole, the gay man stuck a hatpin through it and went upstairs and told the policeman, "Your friend is waiting for you."

This version is especially interesting given the different theme. As a study in revenge it served a cohesive function during the ultrarepressive McCarthy era.

11. R. D. Fenwick, *The Advocate Guide to Gay Health* (New York: E. P. Dutton, 1978), p. 71.

12. Interview with Marc Henderson, 18 November 1981.

13. Esther Newton, *Mother Camp: Female Impersonation in America* (Chicago: University of Chicago Press, 1972), p. 2.

14. Vito Russo, *The Celluloid Closet: Homosexuality in the Movies* (New York: Harper & Row, Publishers, 1981), p. 228. One frequently encounters this line. As Marc Henderson said, "Oh yes, Miss Thing. I'm twice the man you'll ever be and twice the woman you'll ever have." Bob Schultz (accidentally reversing the verbs) gave the line an extra humorous twist, saying, "I'm more man than you'll ever have and more woman than you'll ever be." On the record album *Queen for a Day!* (Union, N.J.: Half and Half Records, LP 34 ½, ca. 1958), Ty Bennett has the following exchange with a member of his audience:

Voice: Hey, come on! You're not a real woman!

Bennett: Not a real woman?

Voice: Naw!

Bennett: Are you kidding? I'm probably more of a man than you are and more of a woman that you'll ever get. Or have.

In *Mother Camp,* Esther Newton reports a similar exchange between a female impersonator and an audience member:

> The performer was attempting to talk to a lady in the audience whom I could not see, and referred to her date as "that fat man you're with." The man shot back, "We'd get along a lot better if you'd address me as 'sir.'" This obviously angered Tris, who retorted, "You paid a dollar to come in here and watch *me*; you'd better believe I wouldn't pay a dime to watch you roast in hell."
> The man wouldn't give up, but repeated his demand, whereupon Tris replied with

elaborate sarcasm in his voice, "Sir . . . ? I'm more 'sir' than you'll ever be, and twice the broad you'll ever pick up." (p. 66)

15. Julia P. Stanley, "Gay Slang/Gay Culture: How Are They Related?" (paper read at the 1974 annual meeting of the American Anthropological Association, in the collection of the Alfred C. Kinsey Institute for Research in Sex, Gender, and Reproduction, Indiana University Bloomington), p. 16.

16. A straight woman telling the joke in a straight context added the line, "And I don't know how many hares."

17. A variant answer heard about the same time is, "Because a cunt would look awfully silly flapping in the wind."

18. Interview with Rebecca Armstrong, 1 April 1981. Compare with Marc Henderson's statement, "I think it's very important to have straight people" (interview, 18 November 1981).

19. Interview with Ramona Halston, 24 March 1981.

20. Interview with John Herrick, 3 December 1981.

21. Compare with the following joke told by Bette Midler in the movie *The Rose* (1980):

Did you hear about the Polish lesbian?
She only liked men.

22. Carol A. B. Warren, "Women among Men: Females in the Male Homosexual Community," *Archives of Sexual Behavior* 5 (1976): 161–62.

23. Ibid., 168.

24. Charles Silverstein and Edmund White, *The Joy of Gay Sex* (New York: Simon and Schuster, A Fireside Book, 1977), p. 52; see also Joan Luxenburg, "'Fag Hags': Peripheral Members of the Gay Community" (paper read at the 1979 annual meeting of the Society for the Study of Social Problems, 1979, in the collection of the Alfred C. Kinsey Institute for Research in Sex, Gender, and Reproduction, Indiana University Bloomington); Rebecca Nahas and Myra Turley, *The New Couple: Women and Gay Men* (New York: Seaview Books, 1979), p. 162; and Robert G. Leger and Diane E. Taub, "Social Identities and the Young Gay Community: The 'Drag Queen'" (paper read at the 1978 annual meeting of the American Anthropological Association, in the collection of the Alfred C. Kinsey Institute for Research in Sex, Gender, and Reproduction, Indiana University Bloomington).

25. Interviews with Michael Monroe, 1 December 1981, and Bob Schultz, 3 December 1981.

26. Interview with Marc Henderson, 18 November 1981.

27. See Newton, *Mother Camp,* passim, and Hector Simms, "A Biopsy on Miss Thing: A Drag Is a Drag," *Gay,* 1 June 1970, p. 15.

28. Interview with Darla Lee, 2 May 1981.

29. Interview with Sabrina Focks, 28 March 1981.

30. See Dennis Altman, *Homosexual: Oppression and Liberation* (New York: Outerbridge & Diestfrey, 1971), p. 18; Paul H. Gebhard, "Homosexual Socialization," *Excerpta Medica International Congress Series No. 150* (Madrid: Proceedings of the IV World Congress of Psychiatry, 1966), p. 1030; Desmond Morris, *Manwatching: A Field Guide to Human Behavior* (New York: Harry N. Abrams, Inc., 1977), pp. 18–19; and Kenneth Plummer, *Sexual Stigma: An Interactionist Account* (London: Routledge & Kegan Paul, 1975), p. 168.

Lesbians interviewed by Greer Trotter Warren identify a similar stage in homosexual women's coming-out experiences:

S: You know what, though, I think the younger gay women are dykier, coming out dykier than the older women.
A: But that's when you first come out, because after you've been out for a while . . . .
S: Yeah, maybe they'll go back.
A: They go back to being ordinary.

(From "Silence Keeping: Conversations with Two Lesbians," unpublished manuscript, 1981, in author's possession.)

31. Interview with Michael Monroe, 1 December 1981.

32. Interview with Marc Henderson, 18 November 1981.

33. Interview with Richard Kennedy, 7 December 1981.

34. The terms *etic* and *emic* were derived by Alan Dundes from the work of linguist Kenneth Pike. *Etic* refers to an outsider's point of view, and *emic* describes the point of view of an insider. See Alan Dundes, "From Etic to Emic Units in the Structural Study of Folktales," in *Analytic Essays in Folklore,* ed. Alan Dundes (Bloomington: Indiana University Press, 1980), pp. 61–72.

35. Quoted in Sigmund Freud, *Jokes and Their Relation to the Unconscious,* trans. James Strachey (New York: W. W. Norton and Co., Inc., 1960), p. 92.

36. Alan Dundes, "The Crowing Hen and the Easter Bunny: Male Chauvinism in American Folklore," in *Folklore Today: A Festschrift for Richard M. Dorson,* ed. Linda Dégh, Henry Glassie, and Felix Oinas (Bloomington: Indiana University Research Center for Language and Semiotic Studies, 1976), p. 135.

5. O Brave New World

1. Barbara Kirshenblatt-Gimblett, "Studying Immigrant and Ethnic Folklore," in *Handbook of American Folklore,* ed. Richard M. Dorson (Bloomington: Indiana University Press, 1983), pp. 43–44.

2. David O. Arnold, "Subcultural Marginality," in *The Sociology of Subcultures,* ed. David O. Arnold (Berkeley, Calif.: The Glendessary Press, 1970), p. 87.

3. Georg Wilhelm Friedrich Hegel, *System der Philosophie, dritter Teil: Phänomonologie des Geistes* (Stuttgart: 1965), p. 431.

4. Robert Darnton, *The Great Cat Massacre and Other Episodes in French Cultural History* (New York: Basic Books, Inc., 1984), p. 193.

5. Margaret Mead, *Culture and Commitment* (Garden City, N.Y.: Anchor Press/Doubleday and Company, Inc., 1978), pp. 13–91.

6. "Soviets: AIDS from U.S. Lab." *Muncie Star,* 31 March 1987, p. 11, col. 4; see also "Wick: A Losing Battle on AIDS," *Newsweek,* 10 August 1987, p. 6, col. 3; "U.S. Welcomes Soviet Disavowal of AIDS Reports," *Muncie Star,* 3 November 1987, p. 19, col. 1; and "Ann Landers," *Muncie Star,* 4 November 1987, p. 13, col. 6.

7. This material on AIDS jokes is drawn from Joseph P. Goodwin, "Unprintable Reactions to All the News That's Fit to Print," *Southern Folklore* 46 (Jan. 1989): 15–39. Alan Dundes argues that AIDS jokes "will continue to flourish" until a cure for AIDS is found ("At Ease, Disease—AIDS Jokes as Sick Humor," *American Behavioral Scientist* 30:1 [1987]: 72–81). Casper G. Schmidt considers AIDS jokes to be an expression of a fantasy of "mass extermination of a sub-human species" ("AIDS Jokes, or, *Schadenfreude* around an Epidemic," *Maledicta* 8 [1984–85]: 69–74). For additional texts, see Reinhold Aman, "Kakologia: A Chronicle of Nasty Riddles and Naughty Wordplays," *Maledicta* 7 (1983): 275–307, especially pp. 290–91.

8. "AIDS on the Talk-Show Circuit." *USA Today,* 24 October 1986, p. 2D. See also Jan Harold Brunvand, "Watch out for 'AIDS Mary,'" syndicated by United Feature Syndicate for release the week of 16 March 1987, and Gary Alan Fine, "Welcome to the World of AIDS: Fantasies of Female Revenge," *Western Folklore* 46:3 (July 1987): 192–97. The

legend was sent to Ann Landers, and to her credit the columnist recognized it for what it was ("Ann Landers," *Muncie Star,* 30 July 1987, p. 11, col. 5).

AFTERWORD

1. Two preliminary studies of lesbian folklore have been done by graduate students in folklore at Indiana University. See Terence Michael Barbazon, "Collection of Lesbian Verbal and Nonverbal Communication" (1980), and Greer Trotter Warren, "Silence Keeping: Conversations with Two Lesbians" (1981), unpublished manuscripts in authors' possession. Judith Levin at the University of Pennsylvania has also been studying lesbian traditions.

2. I met people from Evansville, Vincennes, Columbus, Washington, Worthington, Greencastle, Terre Haute, Bedford, Mitchell, Stanford, Nashville, Spencer, Indianapolis, Fort Wayne, Muncie, and South Bend, as well as from Chicago and Louisville. These were people who came to visit Bloomington's gay community, not students or people attending meetings at the university. Including persons in the latter two categories would expand the list to cover virtually every community in Indiana, every state in the nation, and many foreign countries.

3. These cities are Indianapolis, Muncie, Vincennes, Anderson, and Fort Wayne, Indiana; Ann Arbor, Flint, and Grand Rapids, Michigan; Chicago, Illinois; Cincinnati, Columbus, Toledo, and Piqua, Ohio; Minneapolis, Minnesota; Huntsville, Alabama; Washington, D.C.; Louisville, Kentucky; Atlanta, Georgia; and New Orleans, Louisiana.

4. Kenneth E. Read, *Other Voices: The Style of a Male Homosexual Tavern* (Novato, Calif.: Chandler & Sharp Publishers, Inc., 1980), p. xiv.

5. Norine Dresser, "'The Boys in the Band Is Not Another Musical': Male Homosexuals and Their Folklore," *Western Folklore* 33 (1974): 217.

6. Alan P. Bell and Martin S. Weinberg give succinct descriptions of various aspects of gay social life in "Ethnography of the Bay Area Homosexual Scene," Appendix A of *Homosexualities: A Study of Diversity among Men and Women* (New York: Simon and Schuster, A Touchstone Book, 1978), pp. 233–63.

7. Alan Dundes, "From Etic to Emic Units in the Structural Study of Folktales," in *Analytic Essays in Folklore,* ed. Alan Dundes (Bloomington: Indiana University Press, 1980), pp. 67–68.

8. Zora Neale Hurston, *Mules and Men* (New York: Harper & Row, Publishers, 1970), pp. 18–19.

9. In "The Field Study of Folklore in Context" (in *Handbook of American Folklore,* ed. Richard M. Dorson [Bloomington: Indiana University Press, 1983]), Richard Bauman points out the need for understanding a culture in order to understand the content of its lore (p. 363).

10. Dresser, "The Boys in the Band" and "'What's a Nice Girl like You Doing in a Place like This?': Problems of Conducting Fieldwork in a Homosexual Bar" (paper read at the 1971 annual meeting of the California Folklore Society).

11. Roy D. Smith, "An Exploratory Consideration of Homosexual Folklore" (unpublished manuscript, 1969, in collections of Wayne State University Folklore Archive and Alfred C. Kinsey Institute for Research in Sex, Gender, and Reproduction, Indiana University Bloomington).

12. Roy D. Smith, "Invert Folk Terminology" (unpublished manuscript, 1968, in collections of Wayne State University Folklore Archive and Alfred C. Kinsey Institute for Research in Sex, Gender, and Reproduction).

13. I develop this argument, give definitions of the various forms of language, and substantiate this claim in chapters 1 and 2.

14. Esther Newton, *Mother Camp: Female Impersonation in America* (Chicago: University of Chicago Press, 1972).

15. Drag shows are performances by female impersonators. I discuss them in more detail in chapter 3.

16. Newton, quoting Skip Arnold, pp. 76–77. Bracketed passage in original.

17. Bruce Rodgers, *Gay Talk: A (Sometimes Outrageous) Dictionary of Gay Slang* (New York: Paragon Books, 1979), p. 88.

Selected Bibliography

This bibliography is divided into two sections: a lightly annotated list of works dealing with gay folklore, and a list of other selected relevant resources. Additional references are included in the notes to the text. A complete bibliography is included in the original version of this study: Joseph P. Goodwin, "More Man than You'll Ever Be: Gay Folklore and Acculturation," Ph.D. diss., Indiana University, 1984.

All photocopied, mimeographed, and manuscript materials listed are in the collection of the Alfred C. Kinsey Institute for Research in Sex, Gender, and Reproduction at Indiana University Bloomington unless otherwise indicated.

GAY FOLKLORE RESOURCES

Aman, Reinhold. "On the Etymology of *Gay*." *Maledicta* 3 (1979): 257–58.
  Thought-provoking speculation.
Ashley, Leonard R. N. "*Kinks and Queens*: Linguistic and Cultural Aspects of the Terminology for *Gays*." *Maledicta* 3 (1979): 215–56.
  Detailed (and campy) study of many of the terms used in referring to gay men and their activities.
———. " 'Lovely, Blooming, Fresh and Gay': The Onomastics of Camp." *Maledicta* 4 (1980): 223–51.
  Campy extensive discussion of the relationship between camp terms and camp behavior.
Barbazon, Terence Michael. "Collection of Lesbian Verbal and Nonverbal Communication." Manuscript, 1980, in author's possession.
  List of terms defined by two informants; nonverbal communication is defined. Discussion of variation in lesbian communication.
———. "Drag Shows: Are They Licensed Events for Erotic Display?" Manuscript, 1980, in author's possession.
  Brief description of interaction between female impersonators and their audiences.
Bergengren, Charles. "Folklore of New York City." Manuscript, 1980, in author's possession.
  Includes a few pages on New York City gay folklore.
Brien, Alan. "Camper's Guide." *New Statesman*, 23 June 1967, 873–74.
  "Camp . . . [is] the habit of speaking almost entirely in italics, of tarting up ideas with costume jewellery" [sic]. Proposes that the term comes from late nineteenth-century French *se camper*, "to encamp." Later works have proved the term in its present sense to be much older.
Brunvand, Jan Harold. "Watch out for 'AIDS Mary.'" Column released for week of 16 March 1987 by United Feature Syndicate.
  General discussion of the "Welcome to the World of AIDS" legend.
"Camp and After." *New Statesman*, 4 December 1964, 894–95.
  Denies the connections between camp and gay culture: "There is nothing homosexual in Wilde's comedies," and yet they are pure camp. But camp is "homosexual in nuance if not in action." A rather confused jumble.

Core, Philip. *Camp: The Lie That Tells the Truth*. New York: Delilah Books (The Putnam Publishing Group), 1984.

Excellent encyclopedia of examples.

Cory, Donald Webster [pseudonym of Edward Sagarin], and John P. Leroy. "A Lexicon of Homosexual Slang." In *The Homosexual and His Society: A View from Within*. New York: The Citadel Press, 1963, pp. 261–68.

Glossary containing mostly sexual terms not limited to gay use.

Crew, Louie. "Honey, Let's Talk about the Queens' English." *Gai Saber* 1 (1978): 240–43.

Discusses three forms that gay male English can take: "a greater than average density of items from the male registers of English," "a greater than average density of items from the female registers of English," and "distinctive blends from both registers."

Demakopoulos, Steve A. "The Greek Gays Have a Word for It." *Maledicta* 2 (1978): 3–39.

Discussion of gay argot (*Kaliarda*) in Greece.

Dresser, Norine. " 'The Boys in the Band Is Not Another Musical': Male Homosexuals and Their Folklore." *Western Folklore* 33 (1974): 205–18.

Important because it is apparently the first published work on gay folklore. Perceptive, but misses the important concepts of inversion and defiance, which severely weakens the analysis. Says that with rapid changes in the gay community, this article "may . . . be representative of a way of hidden life soon to become a passe lifestyle." Author's stereotypes are quite clear.

————. " 'What's a Nice Girl like You Doing in a Place like This?': Problems of Conducting Fieldwork in a Homosexual Bar." Paper read at the California Folklore Society meeting. Manuscript, 1971, in author's possession.

Discusses personal and field-work problems of being a straight woman studying the folklore of gay men. Faces up to the stereotypes that are evident in her *Western Folklore* article. "All the difficulties have been external to them, and internal to me."

Dundes, Alan. "At Ease, Disease—AIDS Jokes as Sick Humor." *American Behavioral Scientist* 30:1 (1987): 72–81.

Sets AIDS jokes within a tradition of disaster jokes that serve as coping and distancing mechanisms. Suggests that AIDS jokes will remain popular until a cure for AIDS is found.

Dynes, Wayne. *Homolexis: A Historical and Cultural Lexicon of Homosexuality*. Gai Saber Monograph no. 4 (1985).

The author has a political agenda that is far too intrusive. Much of the work seems to be an attempt to discredit John Boswell's *Christianity, Social Tolerance, and Homosexuality*.

Fennelly, Tony. *The Glory Hole Murders*. New York: Carroll & Graf Publishers, Inc., 1985.

Murder mystery based upon the gay legend.

Fine, Gary Alan. "Welcome to the World of AIDS: Fantasies of Female Revenge." *Western Folklore* 46:3 (July 1987): 192–97.

Interprets the "AIDS Mary" legend as a story of rape and revenge when told by women, of mistrust of women and sexuality when told by men.

Goodwin, Joseph P. "Female Impersonation as a Manipulative Folk 'Genre': The Trickster in Drag." Paper presented at the American Culture Association annual meeting, Louisville, Kentucky, 4 April 1985, in author's possession.

Taking female impersonators as an example, explains how—in the traditional role of the trickster—these performers function as a cohesive force and how they help the subculture cope with conflict. Points out how female impersonation demonstrates the problem of trying to fit gay folklore into the standard genres used by folklorists. Calls into question the value of debating whether *any* folklore is "politically correct."

———. "The Gory Glory Hole." Paper presented at the American Folklore Society annual meeting, Albuquerque, New Mexico, 24 October 1987, in author's possession.

Examines three versions—two gay and one straight—of the widespread legend.

———. "Humour and Conflict in the Gay World." *International Folklore Review* 4 (1986): 96–99.

Discusses role of humor in coping with and defusing conflict within the gay subculture and between gay men and others. The published version was eviscerated; refer instead to the manuscript, "Real Men Don't Use Vaseline: Humor and Conflict in the Gay World."

Grahn, Judy. *Another Mother Tongue: Gay Words, Gay Worlds.* Boston: Beacon Press, 1984.

Interesting speculation on the origins of gay and lesbian culture, although much of the analysis and historical background are not—and probably cannot be—substantiated. Includes a lot of lesbian and gay traditional materials.

Greif, Martin. *The Gay Book of Days.* Secaucus, N.J.: Lyle Stuart, Inc., A Main Street Press Book, 1982.

Daily entries about well-known people reputed to have been gay or lesbian. Notable reclamation of gay history and traditions.

Hayes, Joseph J. "Lesbians, Gay Men, and Their 'Languages.'" In *Gayspeak,* ed. James W. Chesebro. New York: The Pilgrim Press, 1981, pp. 28–42.

Blind acceptance of Julia P. Stanley's "Gay Slang/Gay Culture," q.v.

"The History of the Lambda." *Gaylife,* 27 March 1981, p. 23. Reprinted from *Fifth Freedom,* October 1980.

Traces the meanings of the lambda that make it appropriate as a gay and lesbian symbol.

Jandt, Fred E., and James Darsey. "Coming Out as a Communicative Process." In *Gayspeak,* ed. James W. Chesebro. New York: The Pilgrim Press, 1981, pp. 12–27.

Included here because the title could be misleading. Seeks to develop a "construct" for coming out. Even after reading the article I am not really sure what the authors mean by *communicative process.*

Kelton, Jane Gladden. "A Grammar of Mixed Motives: Masking in the Greenwich Village Halloween Parade." Paper presented at the American Folklore Society annual meeting, Albuquerque, New Mexico, 22 October 1987, in author's possession.

Study of what some have called "the gay national holiday" as it is celebrated in one of the country's largest gay communities.

Knedler, Bryan Keith. "Performance and Power in the Gay Male Community." Master's thesis, Ohio State University, 1983.

Examines one man's use of traditional behaviors to foreground his gay identity, thereby establishing a power base in the Columbus, Ohio, gay community.

Morris, David, and Holly Tannen. "AIDS Jokes and the Folklore of Homophobia." Paper presented at the American Folklore Society annual meeting, Albuquerque, New Mexico, 23 October 1987, in authors' possession.

Examination of how AIDS jokes reflect straight men's conflicting emotions regarding anal intercourse, joking between straights and gays, and changes in AIDS jokes as the disease ceases to be considered primarily a gay problem.

Murray, Stephen O. "Ritual and Personal Insults in Stigmatized Subcultures: Gay—Black—Jew." *Maledicta* 7 (1983): 189–211.

Studies the major themes of ritual insults and the rules of participation in such exchanges.

Newall, Venetia. "Folklore and Male Homosexuality." Folklore 97:2 (1986): 123–47. (Presidential address, [British] Folklore Society, 15 March 1986.)

Survey of traditions of American and European gay men. Much of the material is derived from Joseph P. Goodwin, "More Man than You'll Ever Be: Gay Folklore and Acculturation." Ph.D. diss., Indiana University, 1984.

Newton, Esther. *Mother Camp: Female Impersonation in America.* Chicago: University of Chicago Press, 1972. Reprinted with new preface, 1979.
Cultural anthropological study of female impersonation. Somewhat dated and not altogether accurate. Suffers because of author's lack of esoteric knowledge. Nevertheless, one of the best studies of the genre.

Niemoeller, A. F. "A Glossary of Homosexual Slang." *Fact* 2 (1965): 25–27.
Title is self-explanatory. Such word lists were quite popular in the mid-1960s.

O'Drain, Mary. "San Francisco's Gay Halloween." *International Folklore Review* 4 (1986): 90–95.
Very redundant comment on gay celebration of Halloween in San Francisco, with almost total emphasis on tourists and drag.

Primiano, Leonard Norman. "Normative Religion vs. Vernacular Religion: Notes on the Study of Philadelphia's Gay Catholics." Paper presented at the American Folklore Society annual meeting, Albuquerque, New Mexico, 23 October 1987, in author's possession.
Dignity/Philadelphia serves as a case study of "vernacular" religion, as contrasted with folk, popular, official, and normative religion.

Rodgers, Bruce. *Gay Talk: A (Sometimes Outrageous) Dictionary of Gay Slang.* New York: Paragon Books, 1979. Originally published as *The Queen's Vernacular,* San Francisco: Straight Arrow Books, 1972.
The definitive dictionary of the gay argot; includes etymologies, etymological guesses, and historical notes, as well as examples of usage, sometimes in jokes and anecdotes.

Russo, Vito. "Camp." In *Gay Men: The Sociology of Male Homosexuality,* ed. Martin P. Levine. New York: Harper & Row, Publishers, 1979, pp. 205–10.
Abundant examples convey a feeling for what camp is, but author slips when he claims that "camp . . . is totally apolitical."

Schmidt, Casper G. "AIDS Jokes, or, *Schadenfreude* around an Epidemic." *Maledicta* 8 (1984–85): 69–74.
The author considers AIDS to be "an epidemic of depression, brought about by a conservative swing in American group-fantasy since the middle-Seventies." Within this framework, he maintains that AIDS jokes reflect a wish for mass extermination of gays.

Smith, Roy D. "An Exploratory Consideration of Homosexual Folklore." Photocopied, 1969. Wayne State University Folklore Archive and Alfred C. Kinsey Institute for Research in Sex, Gender, and Reproduction, Indiana University Bloomington.
Rumors that well-known people are or were homosexual. A few jokes and other nuggets. Transcriptions are very hard to follow. No discussion of motivation. Much longer but much weaker than author's "Invert Folk Terminology."

———. "Invert Folk Terminology." Photocopied, 1968. Wayne State University Folklore Archive and Alfred C. Kinsey Institute for Research in Sex, Gender, and Reproduction, Indiana University Bloomington.
Earliest study on gay folk culture that I have found. Detailed interviews with six gay men about argot—vocabulary, acquisition, and use. Insightful discussion, especially for an undergraduate paper.

Sontag, Susan. "Notes on 'Camp.'" *Partisan Review* 31 (1964): 515–30. (Collected in *Against Interpretation.* New York: Delta Books, Dell Publishing, 1967.)
One of the better pieces on camp, but overlooks the serious nature of the style.

Stanley, Julia P. "Gay Slang/Gay Culture: How Are They Related?" Paper read at the American Anthropological Association meeting, 1974.

Argues that *camp* and *closet* and terms derived from them are the only uniquely gay words.

———. "Homosexual Slang." *American Speech* 45 (1970): 45–59.

Claims that the "core vocabulary . . . consists of terms borrowed from the theater and from the slang of prostitutes and the criminal underworld."

"A Vest-Pocket Guide to CAMP." *Life,* 20 August 1965, p. 84.

Brief discussion of camp. Makes some good points.

Vorpagel, Becky. "A Rodent by Any Other Name: Implications of an Urban Legend." Paper presented at the American Folklore Society annual meeting, Albuquerque, New Mexico, 24 October 1987, in author's possession.

Considers versions of "The Colo-Rectal Mouse" that in Philadelphia became associated with a local celebrity and generated a series of jokes.

Waters, Craig. "The Lost World of Emma Jones." *Pensacola Journal,* 26 March 1981, p. 1D.

Created in the 1950s as a name for use on post office boxes where gay men could receive gay literature, Emma Jones became a mythic figure in whose honor annual parties were given until 1974.

OTHER RESOURCES

Achilles, Nancy B. "The Homosexual Bar." Master's thesis, University of Chicago, 1964.

Ackroyd, Peter. *Dressing Up, Transvestism, and Drag: The History of an Obsession.* New York: Simon and Schuster, 1979.

Adair, Nancy, and Casey Adair. *Word Is Out: Stories of Some of Our Lives.* San Francisco and New York: New Glide Publications/A Delta Special, 1978.

Amador, Donald H. G. "Identity and Change in the Los Angeles Male Gay Community." Master's thesis, California State University, 1975.

———. "Water Sports and Other Jargon: The Functions of Gay Terminology." Paper read at the South Western [sic] Anthropological Association, 1974. Photocopied.

Ardrey, Robert. *The Territorial Imperative: A Personal Inquiry into the Animal Origins of Property and Nations.* New York: Atheneum, 1966.

Arnold, David O. "Subcultural Marginality." In *The Sociology of Subcultures,* ed. David O. Arnold. Berkeley, Calif.: The Glendessary Press, 1970, pp. 81–89.

Baker, Roger. *Drag: A History of Female Impersonation on the Stage.* London: Triton Books, 1968.

Bardis, Panos D. "A Glossary of Homosexuality." *Maledicta* 4 (1980): 59–63.

Bascom, William R. "Folklore and Anthropology." In *The Study of Folklore,* ed. Alan Dundes. Englewood Cliffs, N.J.: Prentice-Hall, Inc., 1965, pp. 25–33.

———. "Four Functions of Folklore." In *The Study of Folklore,* ed. Alan Dundes. Englewood Cliffs, N.J.: Prentice-Hall, Inc., 1965, pp. 279–98.

Başgöz, İlhan. "Protest: The Fifth Function of Folklore." Manuscript, 1982, in author's possession.

Bateson, Gregory. "The Position of Humor in Human Communication." In *Motivation in Humor,* ed. Jacob Levine. New York: Atherton Press, 1969, pp. 159–66.

Bauman, Richard. "Differential Identity and the Social Base of Folklore." In *Toward New Perspectives in Folklore,* ed. Américo Paredes and Richard Bauman. Austin: University of Texas Press, 1972, pp. 31–41.

———. "The Field Study of Folklore in Context." In *Handbook of American Folklore,* ed. Richard M. Dorson. Bloomington: Indiana University Press, 1983, pp. 362–68.

Bell, Alan P., and Martin S. Weinberg. *Homosexualities: A Study of Diversity among Men and Women.* New York: Simon and Schuster, A Touchstone Book, 1978.

Bell, Alan P., Martin S. Weinberg, and Sue Kiefer Hammersmith. *Sexual Preference: Its Development in Men and Women.* Bloomington: Indiana University Press, 1981.

Ben-Amos, Dan. "Toward a Definition of Folklore in Context." In *Toward New Perspectives in Folklore,* ed. Américo Paredes and Richard Bauman. Austin: University of Texas Press, 1972, pp. 3–15.

Benedict, Ruth. *Patterns of Culture.* Boston: Houghton Mifflin Company, 1934.

Berry, John W. "Acculturation as Varieties of Adaptation." In *Acculturation: Theory, Models and Some New Findings,* ed. Amado M. Padilla. Boulder, Colo.: Westview Press, 1980, pp. 9–25.

Boswell, John. *Christianity, Social Tolerance, and Homosexuality: Gay People in Western Europe from the Beginning of the Christian Era to the Fourteenth Century.* Chicago: University of Chicago Press, 1980.

Brewer, Joan Sherer, and Red W. Wright, compilers. *Sex Research: Bibliographies from the Institute for Sex Research.* Phoenix: Oryx Press, 1979.

Bronski, Michael. *Culture Clash: The Making of Gay Sensibility.* Boston: South End Press, 1984.

Bullough, Vern L., Barrett W. Elcano, W. Dorr Legg, and James Kepner. *An Annotated Bibliography of Homosexuality.* 2 vols. New York: Garland Publishing Inc., 1976.

Cavan, Sherri. *Liquor License: An Ethnography of Bar Behavior.* Chicago: Aldine Publishing Company, 1966.

Cornelius, David Lee. "An Application of Rules-Based Theory of Interpersonal Communication: The Rules of Taboo Communication within a 'Gay Community.'" Ph.D. diss., Florida State University, 1980.

Cory, Donald Webster [pseudonym of Edward Sagarin, q.v.]. "The Language of the Homosexual." *Sexology* 32 (1965): 163–65.

Dank, Barry W. "Coming Out in the Gay World." In *Gay Men: The Sociology of Male Homosexuality,* ed. Martin P. Levine. New York: Harper & Row, Publishers, 1979, pp. 103–33.

Delph, Edward William. *The Silent Community: Public Homosexual Encounters.* Beverly Hills: Sage Publications, 1978.

Dundes, Alan. "From Etic to Emic Units in the Structural Study of Folktales." In *Analytic Essays in Folklore,* ed. Alan Dundes. Bloomington: Indiana University Press, 1980, pp. 61–72.

Ellis, Albert. *The Folklore of Sex.* New York: Charles Boni, 1951.

Emerson, Joan P. "Negotiating the Serious Import of Humor." *Sociometry* 32 (1969): 169–81.

Fischer, Hal. *Gay Semiotics ♂: A Photographic Study of Visual Coding among Homosexual Men.* San Francisco: NSF Press, 1977.

A Gay News Chronology, January 1969–May 1975. New York: Arno Press, 1975.

Gebhard, Paul H. "Homosexual Socialization." *Excerpta Medica International Congress Series No. 150.* Madrid: Proceedings of the IV World Congress of Psychiatry, 1966, pp. 1028–31.

Gerard, Kent. "Toward Gay History: A Preliminary Bibliography and Provisional Miscellany." Manuscript, 1980, in author's possession.

Germani, Gino. *Marginality.* New Brunswick, N.J.: Transaction Books, 1980.

Glenn, Edmund S., with Christine G. Glenn. *Man and Mankind: Conflict and Communication between Cultures.* Norwood, N.J.: ABLEX Publishing Corporation, 1981.

Goffman, Erving. *Behavior in Public Places.* London: Collier-MacMillan Ltd., The Free Press of Glencoe, 1963.

———. *Frame Analysis: An Essay on the Organization of Experience.* New York: Harper & Row, Publishers, 1974.

———. *The Presentation of Self in Everyday Life.* Garden City, N.Y.: Doubleday Anchor Books, 1959.

————. *Stigma: Notes on the Management of Spoiled Identity*. Englewood Cliffs, N.J.: Prentice-Hall, Inc., 1963.

Grzelkowski, Kathryn P. "Who Am I to Me? Homosexual Self-Identity in a World of Role Versatility." Ph.D. diss., Indiana University, 1976.

Harry, Joseph, and William B. Devalla. *The Social Organization of Gay Males*. New York: Praeger Publishers, 1978.

Harshbarger, Camilla. "Female Impersonation as an Extraordinary Form of Entertainment." Master's thesis, Indiana University, n.d. [ca. 1980.]

Heger, Heinz. *The Men with the Pink Triangle,* trans. David Fernbach. Boston: Alyson Publications, Inc., 1980.

Herskovits, Melville J. *Acculturation: The Study of Culture Contact*. Gloucester, Mass.: Peter Smith, 1958 (reprint of 1938 edition).

Hoffman, Frank A. *Analytic Survey of Anglo-American Traditional Erotica*. Bowling Green, Ohio: Popular Press, 1973.

————. "Institute for Sex Research Folklore File." Manuscript, 1962. (Handwritten entries are periodically added to keep the index up to date.)

Hoffman, Martin. *The Gay World: Male Homosexuality and the Social Creation of Evil*. New York: Basic Books, Inc., 1968.

Holt, Grace Sims. "'Inversion' in Black Communication." In *Rappin' and Stylin' Out: Communication in Urban Black America*. Urbana: University of Illinois Press, 1972, pp. 152–59.

Hooker, Evelyn. "The Homosexual Community." *Proceedings of the XIV International Congress of Applied Psychology*. Copenhagen: Munksgaard, 1961, pp. 40–59.

————. "Male Homosexuality." In *Taboo Topics*, ed. N. L. Farberow. New York: Atherton Press, 1963, pp. 44–55.

————. "Male Homosexuals and Their 'Worlds.'" In *Sexual Inversion*, ed. Judd Marmor. New York: Basic Books, 1965, pp. 83–107.

————. "A Preliminary Analysis of Group Behaviors of Homosexuals." *Journal of Psychology* 42 (1956): 217–25.

Humphreys, Laud. "Exodus and Identity: The Emerging Gay Culture." In *Gay Men: The Sociology of Male Homosexuality,* ed. Martin P. Levine. New York: Harper & Row, Publishers, 1979, pp. 134–47.

————. *Out of the Closets: The Sociology of Homosexual Liberation*. Englewood Cliffs, N.J.: Prentice-Hall, Inc., 1972.

————. *Tearoom Trade: Impersonal Sex in Public Places*. Chicago: Aldine Publishing Company, 1970. Enlarged edition, 1975.

Humphreys, Laud, and Brian Miller. "Identities in the Emerging Gay Culture." In *Homosexual Behavior: A Modern Reappraisal,* ed. Judd Marmor. New York: Basic Books, Inc., 1980, pp. 142–56.

Hymes, Dell. *Foundations in Sociolinguistics*. Philadelphia: University of Pennsylvania Press, 1974.

Jansen, Wm. Hugh. "The Esoteric-Exoteric Factor in Folklore." In *The Study of Folklore,* ed. Alan Dundes. Englewood Cliffs, N.J.: Prentice-Hall, Inc., 1965, pp. 43–51.

Jay, Karla, and Allen Young. *The Gay Report*. New York: Summit Books, 1977.

————. *Out of the Closets: Voices of Gay Liberation*. New York: Douglas, 1975.

Katz, Jonathan Ned. *Gay American History: Lesbians and Gay Men in the U.S.A.* New York: Avon, 1976.

————. *Gay/Lesbian Almanac*. New York: Harper & Row, Publishers, 1983.

Kinsey, Alfred C., Wardell B. Pomeroy, and Clyde E. Martin. *Sexual Behavior in the Human Male*. Philadelphia: W. B. Saunders Company, 1948.

Leger, Robert G., and Diane E. Taub. "Social Identities and the Young Gay Community: The 'Drag Queen.'" Paper read at the 1978 annual meeting of the American Sociological Association. Photocopied.

Legman, Gershon. "Homosexuality and Toilet Inscriptions—An Analysis." Manuscript, 1940–41, Alfred C. Kinsey Institute for Research in Sex, Gender, and Reproduction.

————. *The Horn Book: Studies in Erotic Folklore.* New Hyde Park, N.Y.: University Books, Inc., 1964.

————. "The Language of Homosexuality: An American Glossary." In *Sex Variants,* ed. George W. Henry. New York: Paul B. Hoeber, Inc., 1941, pp. 1149–79.

————. *No Laughing Matter: Rationale of the Dirty Joke,* second series. New York: Bell Publishing Company, 1975.

————. *Rationale of the Dirty Joke: An Analysis of Sexual Humor,* first series. N.p.: Castle Books, 1968.

Lerman, Paul. "Argot, Symbolic Deviance and Subcultural Delinquency." *American Sociological Review* 32 (1967): 209–24.

Levine, Martin P. "Gay Ghetto." In *Gay Men: The Sociology of Male Homosexuality,* ed. Martin P. Levine. New York: Harper & Row, Publishers, 1979, pp. 182–204.

Leznoff, Maurice, and William A. Westley. "The Homosexual Community." *Social Problems* 3 (1956): 257–63.

Licata, Salvatore John. "Gay Power: A History of the American Gay Movement, 1908–1974." Ph.D. diss., University of Southern California, 1978.

Lippmann, Walter. *Public Opinion.* New York: The Free Press, 1922.

Luxenburg, Joan. "'Fag Hags': Peripheral Members of the Gay Community." Paper read at the 1979 annual meeting of the Society for the Study of Social Problems, Boston. Photocopied.

McDavid, Raven I., Jr. "Sense and Nonsense about American Dialects." In *Readings in American Dialectology,* ed. Harold B. Allen and Gary N. Underwood. New York: Appleton-Century-Crofts, 1971, pp. 36–52.

Martineau, William H. "A Model of the Social Functions of Humor." In *The Psychology of Humor,* ed. Jeffrey H. Goldstein and Paul H. McGhee. New York: Academic Press, 1972, pp. 101–25.

Maurer, David W. "The Argot of Narcotic Addicts." In *Readings in American Dialectology,* ed. Harold B. Allen and Gary N. Underwood. New York: Appleton-Century-Crofts, 1971, pp. 500–14.

Maxwell, Robert J. *Contexts of Behavior: Anthropological Dimensions.* Chicago: Nelson-Hall, 1983.

Mead, Margaret. *Culture and Commitment.* Garden City, N.Y.: Anchor Press/Doubleday and Company, Inc., 1978.

Mileski, Maureen, and Donald J. Black. "The Social Organization of Homosexuality." *Urban Life and Culture* 1 (1972): 187–202.

Morris, Desmond. *Manwatching: A Field Guide to Human Behavior.* New York: Harry N. Abrams, Inc., 1977.

Padilla, Amado M. "The Role of Cultural Awareness and Ethnic Loyalty in Acculturation." In *Acculturation: Theory, Models and Some New Findings,* ed. Amado M. Padilla. Boulder, Colo.: Westview Press, 1980, pp. 47–84.

Parker, William. *Homosexuality: A Selective Bibliography of Over 3000 Items.* Metuchen, N.J.: The Scarecrow Press, 1971.

————. *Homosexuality Bibliography: Supplement, 1970–1975.* Metuchen, N.J.: The Scarecrow Press, 1977.

Plummer, Kenneth. *Sexual Stigma: An Interactionist Account.* London: Routledge & Kegan Paul, 1975.

Ponte, Meredith R. "Life in a Parking Lot: An Ethnography of a Homosexual Drive-In." In *Deviance: Field Studies and Self-Disclosures.* Palo Alto, Calif.: National Press Books, 1974, pp. 7–29.

Randolph, Vance. *Pissing in the Snow and Other Ozark Folktales*. Urbana: University of Illinois Press, 1976.

Read, Kenneth E. *Other Voices: The Style of a Male Homosexual Tavern*. Novato, Calif.: Chandler & Sharp Publishers, Inc., 1980.

Rechy, John. *The Sexual Outlaw*. New York: Dell Publishing Co., 1977.

Redfield, Robert, Ralph Linton, and Melville J. Herskovits. "Outline for the Study of Acculturation." In *Acculturation: The Study of Culture Contact*, ed. Melville J. Herskovits. Gloucester, Mass.: Peter Smith, 1958 (reprint of 1938 edition).

Rollins, Joan H. "Introduction: Ethnic Identity, Acculturation and Assimilation." In *Hidden Minorities: The Persistence of Ethnic Identity in American Life*, ed. Joan H. Rollins. Washington, D.C.: University Press of America, Inc., 1981, pp. 1–34.

Royce, Anya Peterson. *Ethnic Identity*. Bloomington: Indiana University Press, 1982.

Russo, Vito. *The Celluloid Closet: Homosexuality in the Movies*. New York: Harper & Row, Publishers, 1981.

Sagarin, Edward [Donald Webster Cory, q.v.]. "Language of the Homosexual Subculture." *Medical Aspects of Human Sexuality* 4 (1970): 37–41.

Sage, Wayne. "Inside the Colossal Closet." In *Gay Men: The Sociology of Male Homosexuality*, ed. Martin P. Levine. New York: Harper & Row, Publishers, 1979, pp. 148–63.

Sonenschein, David. "The Ethnography of Male Homosexual Relationships." *Journal of Sex Research* 4 (1968): 69–83.

———. "Homosexual Humor." *Sexual Behavior* 3 (March 1973): 25–31.

———. "The Homosexual's Language." *Journal of Sex Research* 5 (1969): 281–91.

———. "Patterns of Homosexual Friendships." Master's thesis, Indiana University, 1968.

Spradley, James P., and Brenda J. Mann. *The Cocktail Waitress: Woman's Work in a Man's World*. New York: John Wiley & Sons, Inc., 1975.

Stahl, Sandra K. D. "The Personal Experience Narrative as Folklore." *Journal of the Folklore Institute* 14 (1977): 9–30.

———. "Personal Experience Stories." In *Handbook of American Folklore*, ed. Richard M. Dorson. Bloomington: Indiana University Press, 1983, pp. 268–76.

[Strait, Guy, ed.] *Dictionary of Gay Words and Phrases (The Lavender Lexicon)*. San Francisco: Strait and Associates, 1964.

Toelken, Barre. *The Dynamics of Folklore*. Boston: Houghton Mifflin Company, 1979.

———. "Folklore, Worldview, and Communication." In *Folklore: Performance and Communication*, ed. Dan Ben-Amos and Kenneth S. Goldstein. The Hague: Mouton, 1975, pp. 265–86.

Troiden, Richard R., and Erich Goode. "Variables Related to the Acquisition of a Gay Identity." *Journal of Homosexuality* 5 (1980): 383–92.

Turner, Victor. "Liminal to Liminoid, in Play, Flow, and Ritual: An Essay in Comparative Symbology." *Rice University Studies* 60:3 (Summer 1974): 53–92.

———. *The Ritual Process: Structure and Anti-Structure*. Chicago: Aldine Publishing Company, 1969.

Walle, Alf H. "Getting Picked Up without Being Put Down: Jokes and the Bar Rush." *Journal of the Folklore Institute* 13 (1976): 201–17.

Warren, Carol A. B. *Identity and Community in the Gay World*. New York: John Wiley & Sons, 1974.

———. "Women among Men: Females in the Male Homosexual Community." *Archives of Sexual Behavior* 5 (1976): 157–69.

Weightman, Barbara. "Gay Bars as Private Places." *Landscape* 24 (1980): 9–16.

Weinberg, George. *Society and the Healthy Homosexual*. New York: St. Martin's Press, 1972.

Weinberg, Martin S., and Alan P. Bell, eds. *Homosexuality: An Annotated Bibliography.* New York: Harper & Row, Publishers, 1972.

Weinberg, Martin S., and Colin J. Williams. "Gay Baths and the Social Organization of Impersonal Sex." In *Gay Men: The Sociology of Male Homosexuality,* ed. Martin P. Levine. New York: Harper & Row, Publishers, Inc., 1979, pp. 164–81.

White, Edmund. *States of Desire: Travels in Gay America.* New York: E. P. Dutton, 1980 (paperback edition: Bantam Books, 1981).

Yerkovich, Sally. "Conversational Genres." In *Handbook of American Folklore,* ed. Richard M. Dorson. Bloomington: Indiana University Press, 1983, pp. 277–81.

———. "Extending the Boundaries of Conversational Genres." Paper read at the 1981 annual meeting of the American Folklore Society, San Antonio. Photocopied, in author's possession.

Young, Katharine. "The Notion of Context." *Western Folklore* 44 (1985): 115–22.

Index